THE
SEVENTH
STEP

BILL SANDS

An Approved Publication of The Napoleon Hill Foundation

Published 2019 by Gildan Media LLC
aka G&D Media
www.GandDmedia.com

Front Cover design by David Rheinhardt of Pyrographx

Interior design by Meghan Day Healey of Story Horse, LLC

Library of Congress Cataloging-in-Publication Data is available upon request

ISBN: 978-1-7225-0107-5

10   9   8   7   6   5   4   3   2   1

To Regina

Acknowledgments

This book could not have been written
if it were not for the many people whose work
makes the Seventh Step Foundation a reality:
my friends still in prison
who serve on our committees,
ex-convicts who give of themselves
freely to help, and squarejohns whose loyalty
and dedication are indispensable.

Author's Note

The stories in this book are true,
but many of the names and
identities have been changed
to protect the innocent.

Introduction

Seven Steps to Freedom
by Mitch Horowitz

This book highlights and reinforces the greatest power inherent within each of us. This power is the "secret," if there is one, to any legitimate program of self-help. With it, progress is not only possible but inevitable. Without out, progress will fail to arrive, even with the best therapies, medications, and programs.

It is: *ravenous hunger for self-change.*

An Arab proverb goes, "The way bread smells depends on how hungry you are." Your hunger determines both your outlook on life and your agency to alter it. That hunger alone will determine what you get of out this book.

Author and ex-convict Bill Sands (1920–1969) wrote *The Seventh Step* in 1967 to describe and prescribe his successful prison fellowship program. The Seven Steps fellowship, which

Sands started in 1963, has led large numbers of ex-felons to better, more purposeful, and more productive lives.

"Some of the released men relapsed into crime," *The New York Times* surmised in 1969, "but overall the program worked well."

Bill Sands' work, like that of another Bill, Bill Wilson, coauthor of *Alcoholics Anonymous*, is not limited to one kind of person facing one kind of crisis, in this case a life of in-and-out incarceration. Although the seven-steps approach was designed by and for prisoners, it can, like other modern fellowship programs, free anyone from perpetual conflict and desperation.

This book and its message are not panaceas or a substitutes for a more just society, or for a society like ours that imprisons too many of its people. (When *The Seventh Step* appeared in 1967, the U.S. imprisoned about 100 out of every 100,000 people; as I write these words in 2018, the rate is about 655 per 100,000, although it has recently been dropping.) Rather, *The Seventh Step* functions as a blueprint for individual revolution, which, in turn, requires helping others get free from lives of crisis.

Here are the steps:

The 7 Steps to Freedom

1. Facing the truth about ourselves and the world around us, we decided we needed to change.
2. Realizing that there is a power from which we can gain strength, we decided to use that power.
3. Evaluating ourselves by taking an honest self-appraisal, we examined both our strengths and our weaknesses.
4. Endeavoring to help ourselves overcome our weaknesses, we enlisted the aid of that power to help us concentrate on our strengths.

5. Deciding that our freedom is worth more than our resentments, we are using that power to help free us from those resentments.
6. Observing that daily progress is necessary, we set an attainable goal towards which we can work each day.
7. Maintaining our own FREEDOM, we pledge ourselves to help others as we have been helped.

Anyone familiar with twelve-step programs will recognize some of the same principles at work here. Like the twelve steps, the seven steps emphasize seeking help from a higher power. In chapter three, Sands describes how he and fellow convicts devised this formula and specifically settled upon the word *power* in step two:

> At first the word "force" crept in and was voted down almost at once. Force was what kept them in prison, force was for the captain of the Yard and his bulls. Anything about God, or the Lord, or the Almighty was out. Prisons are full of agnostics. Of course there are some sincerely religious men in any prison, but it's also true that, for many of the cons who claim to have been "saved" while doing time, religion is a shuck.

Hence, the principles of the seven steps are radically ecumenical. There *is* a need to believe that *something* beyond the motor and cognitive functions of the individual lends invisible help to one's efforts, but no name, faith, or doctrine is prescribed. That's yours to find. Napoleon Hill sometimes called it Infinite Mind.

The seventh step in the title means reestablishing lasting personal freedom, and helping others do the same. But, as

Sands writes, this step was not initially designated as the final one. The steps were reordered to spell the acronym FREE-DOM, according to the first letter of each. At one time, the last step—and the one I personally consider most vital—was *step five*: "Deciding that our freedom is worth more than our resentments, we are using that power to help free us from those resentments."

Deciding that our freedom is worth more than our resentments. That statement captures the sense of hunger I described above. It captures another vital fact of life, too: We cannot eradicate unwanted circumstances or behavioral patterns by sheer will; rather we must *substitute* in their place something—strength, love, honor, freedom—that is more meaningful and deeply treasured than our compulsions.

I love this book's realism. Its true-life characters are hardened, often grim people. Not all of them were transformed. Many were. And within their progress you will be able to see the possibilities of your own.

Mitch Horowitz is the PEN Award-winning author of books including *Occult America* and *The Miracle Club: How Thoughts Become Reality*. Visit him @MitchHorowitz.

Chapter 1

A sign along the road said I was leaving town. Though it was certainly not hot, I began to sweat. My hands were clammy, and from time to time I wiped them on my handkerchief.

The town I had left was Leavenworth. The place I was going to was the Federal Penitentiary. It's about five miles from the town to the prison, which was built on a flat plain that makes it easy for the gun guards in the tower to look out and see anyone who might have made it over the wall somehow. The site was not picked by accident.

The car covered that five miles all too fast for my taste. Within what seemed only minutes of leaving the town of Leavenworth, my escort was driving the car around the big gun tower outside the prison gates. He parked and turned to me.

"Come on," he said. Neither of us wanted to talk. One never does, on the way to a prison.

We walked to the foot of the gun tower, and my escort, using the microphone there, talked to the gun guard above and told him who I was. They were expecting me, all right. A loudspeaker told us to go up the main steps. I went first, my escort close behind. There were sixty steps in all. I counted. Each step was like a punch in the ribs to me. It had been years since I had done anything as hard as this. I thought of turning around and bolting, but they were waiting for me in there. I went on.

At the top of the stairs we went through a door into a small anteroom with hard-backed benches. They looked like solid mahogany. At the end of the anteroom I saw a set of iron bars, toward which I walked. Behind them was a big circular cage of glass—green glass, thick glass, obviously bulletproof glass. A lone guard sat in it.

The guard in the outside tower must have told him I'd arrived. The one inside the glass cage pulled a lever, and the gate that was set in the iron bars opened to let me through. I was facing another mike and loudspeaker and a round aluminum table, half in and half out of the glass cage. The caged guard rotated the table so that the pad and pencil that had been on the inside were now outside, with me. The loudspeaker told me to register.

I wasn't in and I wasn't out. I was in an area that lay between one set of iron bars and another, with the bulletproof glass at one side. I wrote down my name and address and all the other statistics and details the form called for. The table turned again, and now the paper was inside the cage.

The guard spoke into an intercom. I couldn't hear what he said. I had nothing to do but wait there between the glass cage and the bars. I looked up, expecting to see an electronic frisking machine that searches you for metal, a knife, anything like that. If there was one I couldn't detect it.

A prison official came out and told me who he was. I told him who I was. Then I thought that that was a thing only a very nervous man would do. He already knew.

He nodded at the guard in that ghastly fishbowl, and we walked around to the next gate. It opened and we went through, and electronics snapped it shut with a loud clang behind us. I was in prison, behind more steel bars than the meanest animal in the zoo. I could feel myself trembling, and I tried to conceal my tension from the officers around me. The man at the controls swung around on his stool, and under his eye we walked to the third gate. It opened, let us through, and closed behind us. This was it.

We were in the rotunda of Leavenworth federal prison then. It is a huge one. Four rectangles of cell blocks go off it, though we could see only the two front ones. There was a faint, barely perceptible smell of antiseptic, and a steady, sullen noise came from the cell blocks, as of many men talking in subdued, tense tones.

The official tapped my elbow and we went through the rotunda and up some stairs, prison iron stairs, up and up. There was a real catacomb of prison iron stairs and prison iron galleries, and I thought I could never find my way back to the fishbowl alone. Not that it would do me any good if I could. I'd never be allowed out. The glassed-in guard wouldn't throw his levers at my request. I was locked in until the guard said to lock me out again.

Finally he opened a door and we were in a small auditorium. There were a hundred and fifty, maybe two hundred men waiting for us there. They were dressed in gray, like most prisoners. It was over twenty years since I'd seen a bunch of convicts, but the sight of them brought it all back. I'd been one of them. I still was.

Then the official with me got up on the platform and started talking about me. I shook off my sick misery and remembered what I was there for. I'd promised to make a speech in this grim place, a speech that would offer hope and guidance to a couple of hundred losers. How this happened is a long story. What I hoped to accomplish by it I couldn't have said then. What I hope I have accomplished, as it turns out, is an even longer story.

While the prison official was introducing me, I found myself reviewing the past. What a long, circuitous road it was that had brought me to this place on this day!

I can't say the home in which I was reared was exactly a happy one—but it was what people speak of as "a good home," with all the "advantages." My father, a superior court judge in California, was in comfortable financial circumstances, and my mother was a beautiful woman whose gracious manners won her the admiration of her social circle. My father had a drinking problem and my parents were separated when I was twelve. To say that my adjustment to being alone with my mother, or her adjustment to being alone with me was poor would be the understatement of the century. Whether my mother was trying to make up to me for the loss of my father's authority or whether she simply hated me, I can't say now. But at the time I was sure she hated me. When she disapproved of anything I did, she beat me. It was her mistake. Instead of mending my ways, I rebelled.

When I was sixteen I committed the ultimate gesture of defiance against her. I invited myself to live with my father, and he accepted me. Mother placed no obstacle in my way—a fact I took as confirmation of her hatred toward me—and father professed himself glad to have me. I didn't believe him. Within months I told him I was running away to sea. That he didn't try to stop me convinced me that he didn't care what I did. The authorities cared enough to have me shipped home when I ran out of money. But by that time I was firmly committed to a career of rebellion and defiance. As I saw it I was going to force the world to take notice of me.

Even so, my first brush with crime was almost accidental. It began with a poker game in which I lost all my money. That was bad enough. Then, after the game, I found the car my father had lent me devoid of hubcaps, radio, and spotlight. At first I was simply trying to make good my losses by stripping other cars. But then I found an old World War I revolver and that spurred me on to bigger games. I pulled five stickups that very night. The revolver couldn't have been fired, but that didn't stop me. My spree of robberies which went on for several weeks, finally landed me in reform school. There I found nothing to alleviate my resentment. The Preston State Reformatory at Ione, California, did little to reform me. I arrived there full of fight, landed myself in solitary confinement in short order, emerged even more full of fight, and escaped. When I returned to Preston to finish my term, The Man (as all adult authorities are called in reform schools) was more determined than ever to break me—and I was more determined than ever not to be broken. It was then that I received my first beating from a correctional officer, and it was then that I stated my declaration of policy—never to conform, never to "sir" an officer, and to get out before I'd served all my time. My father was my ace in the hole. I thought if I embarrassed him enough he'd use his influence to get me released. It worked, and I was released as rehabilitated, a lot more stubborn and more violent than I was when I went in. You might think I would have been grateful to my father, but I wasn't. The way I saw it then, getting me out wasn't something he'd done for me. It was only something he'd done for himself.

When I started on my next string of robberies, only a few months after leaving Preston, I thought I was getting even with everybody—my father, my mother, the reform-school guards, the cops. And this time I really set my mind to it. In only one night's work, my partners and I robbed sixteen places, spread over an area of four counties. I lasted quite a while outside, more than two months. In reform school you learn to keep your mouth shut. I'd learned this—but one partner hadn't. During an accidental encounter with a policeman who had no interest in us at all, he panicked and told all. I had learned to dislike stool pigeons in reform school, but right then I began to hate them. I've never stopped hating them.

There were two important differences between this arrest and the previous one. The first difference—this time I was no longer considered a juvenile nor was I a first offender. The prospect before me was not reform school, but a real penitentiary. And the second difference was that this time, when my father came to jail to talk to me, he succeeded in convincing me that he really did love me and did care what became of me. He wanted to get me out of the jam I'd landed myself in no matter what it cost him. I wouldn't let him. I had my first inkling of what it meant to "ride your own beef," as convicts put it. This was my problem. I knew that his political enemies and the press would crucify my father if I let him solve it for me. Besides, the prospect of serving time in the penitentiary didn't seem so terrible once I could let myself believe my father did love me and would be waiting to help me when I got out. I determined that—once I'd taken my punishment—I'd make myself a son he could be proud of after all.

It was on the 2nd of July in 1941 that I stood in the courtroom and heard Judge Clement D. Nye pronounce my sentence: not less than one year nor more than life in San Quentin. And it was on Independence Day, July 4th, that I arrived at San Quentin to begin serving it. My parting words with my father had nearly broken my heart—when he had to say goodbye to me, I saw for the first time just how badly I had hurt him. He looked old and broken. That haunted me when I entered San Quentin. Only the hope that I could make it all up to my father someday kept me going.

I needed that hope. The prison itself was bleak enough, but the first really bad shock was finding that I was no longer Wilber Power Sewell—only prisoner number 66836. I soon found that fictional representations of prison life were not exaggerated. The prison itself was called the "joint," the guards were sometimes "gun bulls" or "yard bulls," and more often "hacks" or "screws." I learned to call a knife a "shiv" and a gun a "rod," and I learned that the crimes for which I was "busted" were not robberies but "heists." Natural homosexuals were "queens." Other men who were terrorized into performing homosexual acts—or who allowed the indignities for money or advantages—were called "punks." The caste system of a joint was new to me too. The lifers—murderers and multiple offenders—had the best jobs and were, socially speaking, at the top of the heap. Armed robbers ranked high too, because their crimes demanded guts, and even a certain perverse honor. At least they faced their victims directly. Confidence men came next, then burglars, pick-pockets, and purse-snatchers. Lowest on the list were sex deviates. Everyone serving time for sex crimes, regardless of the nature of the crime, was called a "rapo," and every rapo was regarded with the deepest scorn by all the other convicts.

It was in San Quentin that I learned the convict code. The first requirement for any convict who wants to enjoy the respect of his fellows is to be "solid." Among other things, a solid con is one who does not break a promise made to another convict, who will not rat on anyone no matter what the pressure brought to bear by the screws. It was not long before my test came.

Only a few weeks after I entered San Quentin I had the bad luck to witness an incident in the Main Yard that a more experienced prisoner would have known enough to miss. One minute a fellow convict was standing in front of me in perfect health. The next, a prison-made shiv had slit open his abdomen and he lay cruelly wounded at my feet. Worst of all, I had seen clearly the face of the man who wielded the shiv. He disappeared into the more than four thousand men in the Yard in an instant. If I had any sense I would have done the same thing, but I didn't. I stood gawking until the Yard bulls rushed up and surrounded me. They took me to an isolated cell.

I was lucky no one thought I had stabbed the convict. I didn't feel very lucky. I had no idea what had provoked the stabbing, but I did not intend to tell any screw what I knew. So I played dumb. They weren't fooled. Their first questions were polite. So were my answers. Polite but stubborn. I had said I was looking the other way, and I intended to stick to my story. When they saw that persuasion was useless, the politeness dropped away. And for the first time in my life I caught the full brutality that sadistic men in power are capable of inflicting on anyone in their grasp. The first blow seemed enough to kill a man—but then I'd never been hit with a lead-tipped club before. The first blow was nothing compared to those that followed. I have no idea how long it lasted or how many times I passed out, but I do know there were four strong guards, all armed with those leaden clubs, ranged against one unarmed prisoner. And I know I left some teeth in that locked room, and when I left there all the bones and cartilage in my nose had been smashed, and my fingers had been broken one by one.

I don't remember how it ended, but when I woke up I was back in my cell. I hadn't told them who had wielded the shiv, and that made me a solid con.

The screws didn't want me in the hospital—maybe because the doctors would have reported my strange accident to the new warden, who did not approve of such things. So they didn't report me sick, and didn't relieve me of my work assignment in San Quentin's infamous jute mill. For medicine, I had some cold water that my cellmate provided, and his blankets over me to offset the shock I was suffering. Other convicts came into my cell and set my fingers for me as best they could. Some of them are still a little crooked. Men I had never known and never would know smuggled food into my cell, and others performed my task at the jute mill. In time I recovered. I was young and strong.

I took a good look at the two societies I was familiar with. The outside world had produced an alcoholic father and a cold and uncaring mother, and a sadistic prison guard who could break my bones with impunity and then go home and eat his dinner with his family in a house provided by the state.

Then there was the inside world—the convict world. These men in prison gray had nursed me, fed me, done my work for me—and each time a convict helped me, he was inviting for himself the same kind of bone-breaking abuse that I had just been subjected to. Strangers faced those lead-tipped clubs for my sake.

I resolved then and there to join the convict world and to adhere to the convict code. And I became a lifelong hater of sadistic cops.

For my father's sake, I tried to keep my resolution to stay out of trouble, despite my bitterness and the deep need for revenge the screws had bred in me. But I was hardly on my feet after the beating when I suffered the worst blow of all. The screws broke it to me in characteristically compassionate fashion—they handed me a newspaper in which the story was headlined. My father had died.

I don't know what happened to me for a while after that. The time is blurred, until the day I attacked a fellow con and nearly killed him. I do know what happened then—hours and days in solitary (on "the shelf" as San Quentin cons call it). And during those hours and days I knew that I was really lost. I'd been labeled incorrigible before that—from now on I would be. I felt nothing but bitterness and a desire for revenge.

I am a gregarious guy by nature—and solitary was not easy for me. It's all very well to live to get revenge, but in solitary confinement there's nothing on which to be revenged. There is only a tiny cell, a metal bunk, a lidless toilet, and one's self for company. Silence weighed heavily on me. I don't know how long I'd been there—there was no way to keep track of time—when I had a visitor. I was so taken aback I forgot, for a moment, all my hatred, and just sat and stared at him.

I had seen the man at a distance and under the most surprising circumstances. Every place he walked in that prison the convicts would stop whatever they were doing and applaud his progress. The man they were applauding had become warden not long before. He was eliminating graft and brutality from the prison routine and had increased the diet. But above all he was treating convicts as though they were men instead of animals.

For this he was receiving a great deal of adverse publicity. Once a radio commentator interviewing him remarked acidly, "You should know that leopards don't change their spots!" The new warden replied, "You should know I don't work with leopards. I work with men, and men change every day." It was a reply typical of Clinton T. Duffy.

The first thing he did was to ask if I was all right. When I heard the grave, courteous tone of his voice, all the bitterness I felt went out of my mind. To my surprise I heard myself answering in the same polite tone that I was all right. He went on to inquire whether I'd been manhandled in any way. This came as a surprise to me. I had assumed he must know all about it. But he went on to explain that he was opposed to brutality in any form. He suspected, he said, that instances of it still survived from the days before he had taken over San Quentin. For some reason I felt that telling him about the beating I had had would be squealing, and I wasn't going to be a stool pigeon. So even though I hated the screws who had done it, I said I hadn't been manhandled. Whether Warden Duffy believed me or not I can't say, but he dropped the subject. Then I listened to what he had come to say.

He told me, among other things, that the convict I had attacked and almost killed had a subnormal I.Q. and had little chance of coping with the world. I glibly apologized for my action—after all, that's what he was asking for, wasn't it? But he challenged me so soberly that I had to admit I hadn't thought about whether I was really sorry about it or not. I wasn't sorry, either. Not then.

Duffy told me he had no interest in merely keeping criminals out of society. He wanted, whenever it was possible, to help men to ready themselves for freedom. Most prisoners get out of penitentiaries sooner or later. Duffy was concerned more than anything else with what his charges would be like when that happened. "Why don't you try to use your intelligence to work your way out of here?" he said.

I stared at him. Since my father's death I had written my mother many times, begging for some word from the outside. I had never received an answer.

"Why should I?" I answered at last. "Nobody cares about me. Nobody!"

And Duffy looked at me long and steadily and said, "I care."

That was a beginning. When I had chosen to go to prison, rather than use my father's influence to get me out of trouble, I had determined that I'd spend my time in San Quentin well. Now I began to make that determination good. Oh, I wasn't exactly a model prisoner, I wasn't any angel. I was still a solid con—and the other cons knew it. But Duffy wasn't the kind of warden who had any use for stool pigeons or for the kind of man who curries favor with the guards at the expense of other convicts. I managed to keep out of trouble and do my own time without losing my ability to identify with men around me.

In time I worked up to being a prisoner-clerk. The man at the desk next to me was named Caryl Chessman, and we eventually were cellmates and good friends. I served the last months of my sentence at Chino, then California's new minimum-security prison. From there I was paroled, and since then I've spent some twenty years free of crime.

For the most part they've been fine years. I have tried my hand with some success at a variety of things. I was president of two corporations, executive manager of five airports and a hotel for Panagra, a prizefighter in the Philippines, a racing car driver, and an airplane pilot. I ran a dance studio and I prospected for diamonds in Venezuela, and I staged a water show on the Arabian desert. I was also in and out of show business.

It wasn't all rose. Early in my life I married, and it didn't work out. The unhappy years weren't the worst of it. We had a son, and I hated having to leave him when he was only six years old. I knew my wife would remarry, and didn't dare expose the boy to the kind of divided loyalties that had plagued my own childhood. I relinquished all claim on him when my wife and I were divorced. That hurt more than any other thing I've had to do in my life.

It was a long time before I married again. My second wife, Pony, was small, redheaded, and had a compact athletic figure. Pony had a little daughter named Bonnie, whom I came to love as if she were my own. Pony is a fine newspaperwoman who has won many prizes, and her work had brought her close to Caryl Chessman during the long years of uncertainty that preceded his execution. She had been one of the witnesses he had chosen to see him die, and although Chess had made his last gesture one of reassurance to her, his death had hurt her cruelly. Pony and I had both thought highly of Chess, and we both felt that he was innocent of the crime for which he died. It was one of the bonds between us. After our marriage the Chessman execution was one reason we decided to leave California—Pony was having difficulty recovering from the experience.

We settled in Kansas City, where I did a few nightclub turns, set up a sales consultant firm, and got acquainted with my new family. But somehow, changing homes and jobs didn't erase the searing recollection that a friend of ours had been killed in California's gas chamber. It wasn't a thing we talked about a lot, but it was there, in the back of our minds. Maybe it contributed to the restlessness I felt in those early months in Kansas City. I'm not sure, but restless I certainly was. Everything I had ever done for a living had come out all right for me, but nothing had ever satisfied me. I wanted something different from all I had ever done before, but I couldn't tell just what.

Then one night, when I was lying awake, tossing and turning, Pony came up with an idea. I was scheduled to entertain a Shriners' meeting within days, and she suggested that, instead of the usual routine of gags, I talk about something serious for a change, something I really knew. Prison, capital punishment, the fact of being an ex-con—those were the things, Pony said, that I most cared about. She thought she could get the local newspapers interested in such a talk, and it would certainly give the Shriners something different. Best of all, it would be doing something for the memory of Chess and for guys like him who were still alive.

Maybe it was a crazy idea, but I loved it. The talk I gave was certainly unexpected. And surprisingly the audience responded beyond my wildest dreams and so did the press. It was the first time I'd ever aired in public my firm convictions about prison life and I really gave it everything I had. I said our whole system of punishment is based on the concept of revenge—which is why it fails to reduce the crime rate. I said capital punishment is not a deterrent, and that statistics on crime prove this. Homicide is less common in states that have abandoned capital punishment than it is in states that still employ it. I told them that the underlying attitude of society and most penologists and authorities toward the convict is dead wrong, that I, as an ex-con, know more about rehabilitating criminals than most of the experts are ever going to find out. I said something ought to be done about it. I said nobody can ever really understand convicts except someone who has been one. The newspapers reported all of it. That was why I had been invited to Leavenworth to address a group of convicts.

When I agreed to make this Leavenworth appearance, frankly, I had no conception of how hard it was going to be just to walk into the prison, let alone talk to anyone. What's more, I actually didn't know what I was going to say. While the Leavenworth director of education was finishing his introduction, I stared at my audience. A couple of hundred silent grim men dressed in convict gray stared back. I'd forgotten something I once knew well—that prisoners are the best audience in the world if what they're offered is in any way worth hearing.

Prison routine is so monotonous that any break is likely to be welcomed with wild enthusiasm. But these men didn't look very enthusiastic, and in a few seconds I knew why. The director of education was telling them they were about to be addressed by a man who had been a convict "like yourselves." But I knew just what these prisoners were thinking. That I wasn't anything like them. That if I were, no one would let me talk to them. That I must be an ordinary citizen who'd taken one freak fall. That as a convict I had always been the correctional officers' pet. That I might even have been a stool pigeon. That I was going to tell them they had done naughty things and ought to behave in the future. No solid convict would believe that one of his own kind would ever be brought into the prison by the authorities to talk.

When I got up I knew I had to break down that barrier and fast. But how? On my feet, I suddenly knew what to say. "I was introduced," I told them, "as an ex-con, just like you. But I'm not just like you. You guys are stupid. I'm not."

I had accomplished one thing. They were listening. But they didn't look very happy.

"How can I tell you're stupid and I'm not?" I asked them. "Very easily. You're doing time in a joint. I'm free."

Then I told them all the things I hated about joints—cop-lovers and screws and stool pigeons—and all the things I liked about freedom. I told them I'd been incorrigible once—and had managed to stay free for over twenty years since. I told them they could do it too, if they wanted to. And I told them I'd help them if I could.

Afterward they mobbed me. Apparently I was the first guy to talk to them with whom they could identify. Some of those hard convicts had tears in their eyes. I hadn't expected that, and somehow it got through to me. After twenty years of wandering I'd found my calling—though I didn't really know it yet.

Chapter 2

It would be nice to say that I had gone to Leavenworth because my heart ached for those men in prison, but it wasn't so. I was just fooling around as I had been doing all my life—trying this, dabbling with that, driving at something else and being successful at it and then dropping it. Any apparent altruism involved was what the convicts call a shuck—something that looks worthwhile you do for the sake of serving yourself. What was in it for me?

For years I'd heard and read proposals and counter-proposals about crime and criminals, about prevention and rehabilitation, all of which were set forward in solemn tones by experienced professionals. I knew, or thought I knew, what was wrong with all the theories and projects they tried. They had statistics, studies, elaborate rationalizations worked out by doctors and sociologists and psychologists. But they didn't know anything about the men they worked with—convicts. I did. I wanted to prove to the experts how much they didn't know, to show them up. What was in it for me? Perhaps you could call it revenge.

After talking to the Shriners and at Leavenworth, I was invited to appear on several radio shows. On every one I told the same story. I said that—if anyone cared to give me a crack at it—I could show the experts how to reform convicts so they'd stay reformed. Talking about things I really knew made me feel just great. Then I met a newspaperman, Jim Emerson, who ran a paper out in Johnson County, Kansas. He asked me to write a few articles for his paper, articles about crime and the evils of capital punishment, and about the prison system.

One day Jim called me and said the chaplain out at Kansas State Prison, in Lansing, had read the stories and wanted to see me.

His name is the Reverend James E. E. Post, but he said I was to call him Jim. He's a big husky-looking man, and he dresses like a gambling golf player. But I found him absolutely sincere.

All he wanted to know was how he could help get something started that would keep ex-prisoners out of prison as I had kept myself.

I said—more or less off the top of my head—that I'd like to start a prerelease class in prison. Jim Post liked the idea. He promised he would try to get me permission to give it a whirl at Lansing.

Now was the time for me to do some thinking.

How had I stayed out of prison? Why do men go back to prison, time after time, until they die or are too feeble to commit any more crimes? What motivates them?

What I saw was resentment. All cons resent the treatment they got as children—an unfair teacher, an insincere father, a bitch of a mother, or a myriad of other grievances—so they commit an act of defiance. This brings them into conflict with the law—and they resent the treatment they get at the hands of cops, social workers, juvenile authorities.

So then they are started on the endless carousel called recidivism, which is defined as a "sinking back into crime." From first offenders, they become second offenders, multiple offenders, eventually habitual criminals, and every sentence they serve in hatred and resentment. Some are restless to get out, so they can prove again that they are still rebels against a system that is unfair. Others are willing to try to make it honestly—and yet they fail.

This I knew. I had known it ever since I had been a prisoner myself. But how then had I managed to stay out of prison?

The first conclusion I reached was that I had changed enough so that I could prize my freedom more than my resentments.

So far, there was nothing particularly brilliant in my thinking. Why then couldn't other men recognize that freedom was worth more than rebellion, as I had realized? And why couldn't penologists convey that idea to other convicts as Warden Duffy had conveyed it to me? It was there that I thought I had a clue.

I was able to respond to Warden Duffy because of the kind of home I'd come from. Sure, I was classified as incorrigible—a Main Yard tough. But I was also a judge's son. I knew enough about Duffy's official world to recognize his goodness and his honesty when he talked to me. What this means is that when I was willing to do it I could identify with Duffy. Most convicts can never identify with any guard or official, any judge or parole officer or policeman, any social worker or psychologist. The concern or integrity the man who wants to help might show doesn't get through to the convict. There is an invisible barrier, like a glass wall, that descends between honest citizens and convicts, and it makes the average con stone-deaf when anyone from the non-criminal world tries to reach him.

I reasoned that there might be one exception to this rule. I thought that possibly an ex-con could reach convicts on their own terms, talk to them in their own language. Knowing how they see things, possibly he could do what no professional could do for them. That was what, instinctively, I'd tried to do at Leavenworth. And my reward there was the sight of tough cons crowding around me with tears in their eyes. If my desire to put down the cops and guards and experts hadn't been motivation enough for me to want another round, the sight of those Leavenworth cons would have clinched it.

Lansing sounded to me like a good place to start. It was reputed to be one of the country's many very bad prisons. It is a grim place. It was built a hundred years ago in the style of the time, which decreed that penitentiaries and breweries should both look like German castles. But there is nothing Rhenish about that flat, desolate prairie that is the site of Kansas's prison. The place is gray and, like almost all prisons, overcrowded. It is chilly in winter and stifling in summer. Penitentiaries are so named because they were originally intended to make the men in them repent. But resentment, rather than repentance, is what you get when you throw men into a place like Lansing.

The guards at Lansing match the building. They have to. They aren't paid a modern wage, and they have little future beyond the dreary possibility of being promoted to officer of guards. If a program could succeed there, it could succeed in any prison anywhere, no matter how discouraging conditions might seem.

When Jim Post had offered to help me found a prerelease class, I had told him that I wanted the chance to work with *every* man who was within four months of his release—not with the custodial staff's hand-picked pets. I also wanted one chance to talk to the eighteen hundred men who compose the entire prison population. Jim helped me win approval from the Director of Penal Institutions for the state of Kansas, Robert J. Kaiser, and from the warden at Lansing, Sherman H. Crouse.

For my one appearance before the whole population I decided to get their interest aroused by starting out with my nightclub act. I had the authorities announce that, for the first time in Lansing history, a professional entertainer was being brought in to entertain the men in the prison auditorium after the Saturday-afternoon movie.

Pony, Jim Emerson, and Jim Post notified all the news media of our plans and arranged a press conference, to be held beforehand, and news coverage of the speech itself.

Then I had an idea. I knew Warden Crouse would have to deny me permission to carry it out, so I began what I can only call an end-run around him.

The first step was to get a press pass for my wife, Pony. That wasn't hard. She wasn't working then, but she had been on the Hearst papers for years, and might well be expected to want to write a story about the evening at Lansing.

Women had never been admitted inside the walls at Lansing, but since the inmates would all be watching the movie during the press conference, Warden Crouse agreed that Pony might go as far as the officers' dining room, where we were meeting the reporters.

When the press conference was over it was time for me to get on with the show, so all the reporters trooped up to the auditorium in a group. Pony trooped right along with them.

Warden Crouse, of course, thought he had just given Pony a pass to the officers' dining room. The guards may have thought he had given her permission to sit on the stage with me. Actually, I'm not sure what the guards thought. After all, they are more accustomed to keeping people in than out.

Where she was going, where I was going to place her, was right in the middle of the eighteen hundred convicts on the auditorium floor. We got away with it. Pony is a small women—perhaps that helped.

I had rehearsed the prison band thoroughly the day before, and they did a good job. I ran through a typical nightclub routine of songs and patter, and it went over just fine. Now it was time to stop being an entertainer, time to introduce myself as an ex-con who was there to show other cons how to stay out of prison.

This was ticklish work. I didn't want them to think that I had staged the entertainment as a means of trapping a captive audience into listening to a sermon. But I did want to let every man in the prison know who I was and what I was there for. When I told them I was there as an ex-convict, they listened, but I could feel right then that they were skeptical. Like the men at Leavenworth, they were sure they knew exactly what kind of screw-loving, stool pigeon ex-prisoner would be allowed to talk to them.

So I plunged fast. I began even more forcefully than I had at Leavenworth. I said, "I'm not the same kind of guy you men are, because you're stupid. You are spending your lives taking orders from men whose collar size is higher than their I.Q.

"I'm not saying," I went on, "that every guard in this joint can take off his shirt without unbuttoning the collar. I'm just saying there aren't many guys who'd take a job as a screw in this joint, at the money they're paying screws, if they had any brains.

"Why be a prison guard? Maybe to get your hands on authority your family and friends don't give you on the outside. Real authority, life-and-death authority.

"And over whom? Over guys too dumb to stay out of places like this.

"Maybe all the screws don't fit my description," I said. "But those who do can put on the shoe and damn well wear it."

The men on the floor, the men in gray, gasped. They had never heard anything like this from anybody but each other. Then they erupted into a spontaneous burst of applause and cheering.

When they quieted down, I went on, "I gather you guys have noticed that I don't like prison guards." That got a laugh. "Well, I've got a surprise for you. There are quite a lot of you I don't like, either. Some of you guys are stool pigeons, and those of you who are, are worse than the guards who are keeping you here. I'm not here to talk to stool pigeons, or cop-lovers. I want to talk to those of you who are solid convicts, the guys who know the answers, the wise ones.

"I didn't think I was stupid when I was a con. I thought I was a wise guy. But now I know different. Every 'wise guy' I know is in prison or on his way to prison.

"You wise guys call any outsider a squarejohn—you think it means sucker. Just stop and think about how the 'sucker' lives. He goes home at night, has a couple of drinks if he wants to, a steak when he feels like it. When he goes to bed he turns off his own light. At the same time, you penitentiary bigshots are being locked in a cell where it's never dark, taking orders from a prison guard, and eating the slop they dish out to you.

You're not even trusted with a toilet seat because they're afraid you'll make a weapon out of it!"

I looked around the stage. I could tell that Warden Crouse had spotted Pony down in the auditorium. He was glowering at me, and it was not because of what I had said about his guards. I had cleared that with him. The guards were glowering too, but they couldn't shoot me. I wasn't wearing prison gray.

I wound it up fast then. "I'm here to show you men how you can get what I've got—a self-respecting place in society, a car, a drink when you want it, a steak dinner that you've earned—and a lovely wife like mine!"

I pointed my finger at Pony, and she stood up and the place went wild. The fact that I had trusted those eighteen hundred men enough to place my wife in their midst really got to them. No one ever shows that kind of faith in a bunch of maximum-security cons.

I'm not sure the warden has ever quite forgiven me. At the time, he didn't understand that Pony was the safest person in the place. He thought putting her in that auditorium was terribly dangerous.

But when I had finished, a lot of the men were ready to sign up for the kind of class I had been talking about.

And that was what I was there for.

Chapter 3

Before I had plunged into what a friend called my "prison-talking business," I had had a pretty good income from my sales work to support Pony and Bonnie. Bonnie had her own horse, and we owned a comfortable home in the suburbs. But my work was full-time—and as soon as I began to develop a regular prerelease program I saw that it would take a full working week. I would have to choose either the program or my income. It seemed crazy to think of working full time for a bunch of convicts when there wasn't a dime in it for me. Besides, it was only a shuck, wasn't it?

Well, I suppose it was, but there was something else too. I'd told those guys in Lansing, eighteen hundred of them, that I was a solid con, that I knew how to help them, and that I was going to do it. They knew and I knew that a solid con doesn't break his word when another convict is depending on him. So if I had to drop everything else to keep my promise, then that's what I should do.

I had never had any trouble getting work or making money. It would only be for a couple of months, I told myself. Just long enough to get things going. I didn't know if it was fair to my family, but Pony had a solution to the problem of money—she suggested that I write a book about my life. When I decided to do as she suggested, I believed that the royalties would compensate for my lost income. And Bonnie clinched the thing when she asked if I wouldn't please let her contribute by selling her horse.

The work of writing was unfamiliar and it was hard too, but Pony helped with it. At least it was work I could do in whatever hours I chose, late at night and on weekends.

So I freed myself for all-day work at Lansing. I needed the time too. Chaplain Post lent me his office, and all day every day I conducted individual interviews there, gathering material to use in my brand-new prerelease class, which was meeting for two hours every Monday night.

After the success of my talk the prisoners were not reluctant to come and see me. We talked alone, as Warden Crouse had arranged, with a single guard out of earshot on the other side of the closed office door.

Convicts are reluctant to trust anyone from outside, however solid he may appear, but I was in luck—there were a few of my old friends from San Quentin serving time in Lansing. One of these, Buck Rogers, was even helping out as my clerk. When old friends passed the word that I had been solid, the men opened up freely to me. Even so, I was not entirely pleased. What I had been hoping to hear about was problems they expected to face on the outside. Not one single man brought such problems. Instead, one after another, men came in with gripes about the rotten food, the stupid or brutal guards on the staff, the homosexuality, and the relentless atmosphere of violence that pervaded prison life. I heard a great deal about incidents inside Lansing, some of them so unbelievable that I took the time to check the records. They were substantially true.

At worst, as the men made clear, the tension and constant possibility of violence in prison can be enough to make murderers out of many convicts who would never kill under ordinary circumstances. This did not surprise me. I almost killed a man in San Quentin.

Killings in prison may take place over anything or nothing. At Lansing, as at many prisons, poker games are a common cause of violence. The authorities try to control the consequences of the widespread gambling—which is supposed to be against the rules but, as everyone knows, goes on anyway—by a system of protective custody that works like this. An inmate gets into a poker game with a really tough con—let's call him Lefty Boyd—and he loses seven dollars, and he can't pay it. He goes to the captain and says, "I owe Lefty Boyd seven dollars and he's going to kill me."

The captain calls Lefty in and says, "This guy says he owes you seven dollars, Lefty." And Lefty says, "Aw, captain, for Christ's sake, we're all square. He don't owe me nothing."

Then the captain puts the inmate in protective custody so Lefty can't get at him. But he turns the inmate loose from protective custody long enough to go out and gamble in the next poker game, and the next, in the hope that he can get his money back. The captain takes this gamble because the poker game is in the middle of the Yard, where the captain has enough stool pigeons to discourage Lefty from killing anyone. There's just one hitch—there isn't anybody who gets money back from Lefty Boyd in Lefty Boyd's poker game. So the inmate either spends the rest of his sentence in protective custody—or he trips and falls on his own knife. That happened to one inmate who owned Lefty Boyd some money. As he left the poker game he tripped and fell on his own knife. He was found with his own hands on it. It was a pretty odd thing because he was a good basketball player, a well-coordinated man. Nobody could understand it.

At Lansing, the victims of knifings are among the luckier ones. The convicts have devised worse ways to kill, and the guards haven't yet found a way to stop them. The fact that this happens might seem unbelievable to anyone who does not know what prisons are like or how they're run. But here are two incidents—both a matter of record—that occurred quite close together at Lansing and haven't been solved to this date. I don't know who committed them, but I do know that the convicts were acting under the peculiar pressure a place like Lansing creates.

We'll call the aggressor Scarface. Let's say that Scarface had asked another convict to hold something valuable for him and the other convict had lost it. (Convicts often get friends or followers to hold property for them, because they're subject to shakedown if the guards suspect they have anything of value in their cells.) Scarface was pretty angry when he didn't get his property back.

Now, in the cell house in Lansing, as in many prisons, a guard is in charge of every cell block. Most cell blocks are five tiers high, and each cell door has a lock on it. Aside from the individual locks, there's a big lock at the end of each tier that locks every cell on the tier. But that one is only used at special times. During the night, for example, when all the convicts are in their cells and sure to stay in their cells, the big lock is used. At other times only the individual locks are used because some men have to enter and leave their cells from time to time for various purposes. In order to keep up with all the errands that might be required, the guard in charge of the cell block might have to climb up three or four tiers to let each man out of his cell and then back in again a dozen or more times. So the guards appoint a convict runner for each tier, and each runner carries the keys to the individual locks.

The runners, being convicts, are subject to all the pressures that the convict population can bring to bear. So a really tough con, a leader in the Main Yard, which we'll have to assume Scarface was, can do anything with the runner he wants. He can have himself let out when other men are out—so that he will not be the only possible suspect—and when his intended victim is locked in. This Scarface did.

Then he put a pillowcase with slits cut for his eyes over his head. He couldn't be recognized by any of the cons who might be watching. He made his way to his victim's cell with a big can of naphtha that he'd smuggled in from the license-plate factory.

The guard sitting at his post at the end of the ground floor couldn't see any of this from his chair. There is no place a guard can sit that offers a clear view into all the cells at one time—there is always a blind spot.

Scarface threw the whole gallon of naphtha into his victim's cell, set fire to a pack of matches, and threw it in after the naphtha. Then he went back to his own cell and got rid of the pillowcase while his enemy burned.

Whether it was the same convict or someone else who liked the idea no one knows, but a couple of months later another convict went exactly the same way, horribly burned with naphtha, alone in his cell, locked in. It's the kind of thing that makes an impression in convict life. Among the tougher cons a lot of guys think the rule is "kill or be killed," and when tensions are running high enough, they're sometimes right.

A Main Yard leader we'll call Foursquare Smith used to run the hottest poker game in the Yard. A fellow convict owed him money, couldn't pay it, and got scared. He wasn't the type to go for protective custody, so he decided the best way to get rid of a creditor who might—just might—kill him was to get his licks in first. He got hold of a big syringe, filled it with sulfuric acid, and then hid in a doorway just off a corridor along which he knew Foursquare would be coming. When Smith was almost on top of him, he just stepped out and—without even saying anything—squirted the acid right in Foursquare's face.

No convict gets to be a Main Yard leader by being stupid. Besides a pretty sharp intelligence, anyone who arrives at that position and stays alive develops an animal-like reaction that you don't find in ordinary life. Foursquare saved himself because he knew there was a place with running water just down a little stairway behind him, only about five feet away. When the acid hit him in the face, he just turned and dived down the stairway. He couldn't see, but he knew where it was. He rolled all the way down and broke his wrist in the process, and then scrambled up and felt his way into a big laundry tub, turned on all the water, and got his face down in it. He saved his sight and wasn't even scarred.

The convict who did it came off pretty well, too. He lived for about four months. Even if a Main Yard leader doesn't take revenge himself, he has a few friends around.

In a lot of prisons, including Lansing, the atmosphere of violence is so strong that killings or attempted killings occur over trifling matters. Homosexual quarrels are fairly commonplace and sometimes fatal. But there are killings over unpaid debts of cigarettes or candy bars. A man who is full of resentment does not make the punishment fit the crime. He will kill because he cannot stand the idea that other prisoners know he has been made a sucker. And there are killings that occur for no reason at all. A man who wants to become a prison bigshot may kill someone—usually but not always someone who already is a bigshot—just to make an impression. I'm not implying that a killing or a stabbing occurs every week or every month in any prison. What I am saying is that the possibility of violence is always there. Convicts hate the threat of violence and the fear, just as anyone would hate it. But brutality becomes a vicious circle. Once involved in it a man sees no way out.

All this was certainly a part—a dreadful part—of life in Lansing, but it was not what I wanted them to tell me about. I wanted the men to bring me questions about the problems they expected to face once they got out, so that I could organize my talks to the class around the things outside they were worried about. Hearing their fears and complaints about life on the inside was getting me no place fast.

There were nearly a hundred men in my class at the time, and for our meetings we gathered in a small, unventilated room, which seemed to be the only place available. There were all kinds of men in that class—a fellow with a Ph.D., and a couple of them who could hardly write their own names. One of them was a real curiosity, the only schoolteacher I can ever remember hearing about in a prison. And he wasn't really a teacher when he took his fall—he had risen to be a superintendent of schools.

At the other end of the scale from that teacher was Wash Carver, whose cellmate had taught him how to sign his name. He was black, short, and built like a tank. If his legs had been in proportion to his shoulders he would have been a good foot taller.

There was a fellow called Pegleg in the class. He was thin, bald, and had a crude wooden leg. Then there was Marble, so named because he had a glass eye. In a hot argument he'd pop it out into his hand, a gesture which usually had a devastating effect on his opponent.

About half the class were clean-cut young fellows. In nicely tailored suits, they could have been mistaken for young dentists, graduate students in a university, junior executives.

For several weeks I had kept these men interested by telling them about problems I had faced on the outside, what they might expect to face, and how they might deal with their problems successfully. I had tried to make my talks entertaining as well as useful. The men's attendance there was voluntary.

One Monday, as I stood before these gray-clad men, with their hard faces turned toward me, I began by saying, "For the last several weeks I've been up here every Monday night telling you guys what life is like on the outside. And the rest of the days of the weeks you guys have been coming to the office and telling me what life is like on the inside.

"I've heard your bitches and I've heard your beefs and I've heard your tales of woe and misery. Now I'm going to tell you guys something and I'm going to tell it to you one time. I don't particularly give a damn about what your life is like inside this prison.

"If I stood up here and talked about the things you've been telling me, I'd be running a class teaching you guys how to be good convicts. But that's not why I'm here. I'm here to teach you guys how to be ex-convicts—and how to stay that way. So I'm not going to listen to any more of your beefs about what goes on inside this prison.

"Now let's get down to the business we came here for."

I spent the rest of the time talking about problems an ex-convict has to face, and dragging out of them questions and misapprehensions about life on the outside. It helped a little, but they were still not cooperating the way I'd hoped.

In the interviews during the week that followed, I still heard nothing I could use in the class. Then one day a convict named Henry Cockerham, who worked in the educational department and was known throughout the penitentiary as a solid convict, asked to talk to me.

"Bill," he said, "I'm not eligible for your class because I'm doing natural life. But I think I can help you."

"How?" I asked.

"I think I know what you're trying to do. You're trying to get a guy's thinking straight before he hits the street. I also think I know what your problem is—you're having trouble getting guys to level with you, to talk about their own problems. Right?"

"Go on."

"Well, I've got a good rep on the Main Yard. Good enough, I think, so I could get a lot of guys I know who *are* in your class to get up in front of the whole group and really tell what they think about getting out. Are you interested?"

Not only was I interested, but I asked Henry to serve as a second full-time assistant. Of course, it had to be cleared with the warden for Henry to change his work assignment, and Henry suggested that while I was talking to Warden Crouse I should ask him if it was possible to make whatever was said in that class privileged, in the way that communications with lawyer are privileged. "Otherwise," he said, "the guys who plan to go on the take when they go out won't talk about it."

"Would Crouse keep such a promise if he made it?" I asked.

"Absolutely," Henry said.

"Would the other guys believe that?"

"Those who know Crouse will from the very beginning, and the others will find out."

I went to Warden Crouse. Not only did he agree to everything I asked, he suggested that if I could find a few other men like Henry Cockerham to assist me, he'd gladly assign them to me too.

It worked.

At the very next class the atmosphere was changed. Henry had primed a couple of guys to raise their hands and ask for the floor.

The first was none other than Lefty, one of the Main Yard poker players.

"Bill," he began, "I've got a problem."

"Lefty," I answered, "I know enough about your dealings in this joint to say that was the understatement of the year!"

The class laughed. Lefty smiled and continued.

"I don't mean on the inside. I'm talking about my old lady. I been hooked up with this broad for eleven years and she's all right except when she's drinking. Twice when she was drunk, she's turned me in to the cops and got me nailed into this joint. But she's a sexy broad and I'm hung up on her. Now she's shacked up with some bartender. I even hear that she actually married the guy—legal and everything."

"What's your problem?" I asked.

"Well, hell, Bill, how'm I gonna get her back now?"

"Get her back! Your problem was solved the minute she got married. You're a prime example of a guy who doesn't know when he's well off. You got hung up on a stool pigeon. Twice you've served time because of her. If she were a man you'd probably have killed her by now, but because she's a woman you want to be a patsy for the rest of your life. You and guys like you will choose a crime partner with meticulous care. You want somebody you know to be solid. Yet you'll choose a woman with whom you think you're going to spend the rest of your life on the basis of whether or not she's sexy. Or well built, or in fact anything except what kind of person she is. That's pretty damn dumb, and if you guys would pay as much attention to choosing a woman as you do a crime partner you'd be a lot better off."

Five hands shot into the air immediately. The first guy I called on said what was in everybody's mind.

"I been cooped up in this joint for six years. What's wrong with planning on a good-looking blonde when I get out? They're not all stool pigeons."

The man who asked the question, Charlie Mann, was a guy I'd talked to many times in private interviews. He had a fifth-grade education, an I.Q. of about ninety, was almost forty years old, and looked like a third rate garage mechanic, which he was. He had given me a beautiful opening to say something that had been in my mind for a long time.

"Every one of you guys, when you go back to your cell tonight, is going to think about what you're going to do when you get out. That's natural and I don't blame you. But none of you thinks about it like it really is. You, Charlie, are a mechanic. Right?"

He nodded.

"Now I'll tell you what kind of daydreams you manufacture for yourself and what kind of reality you don't face. You don't ever think about yourself as being on a crawler under an old car, with grease dripping in your face and your knuckles skinned from a wrench that slipped and a foreman hollering at you to get the job finished. It isn't any fun to think like that, but that's the way it really is.

"You dream of yourself as being dressed in a nice white service manager's uniform, checking out a minor mechanical problem for a beautiful blonde in a white convertible. And that's not the way it is, and you know it.

"And what about women? All of you guys, when you think about the gal you're going to have when you get out, dream of someone who looks like Marilyn Monroe. You never dream about some ordinary-looking gal, maybe a little overweight, who wears ordinary clothes and leads an ordinary life. Well, I'll tell you something. If you didn't have to beat off the Marilyn Monroes with a club before you came in here, you sure as hell aren't going to have to worry about them when you get out.

"You guys are all short-timers," I continued, "or you wouldn't be in the class. The time has come for you to start thinking realistically about what life is really like on the outside. It hasn't changed any. If the outside world matched your inside dreams, not one of you would return to prison. Even you guys who are planning on going on the take when you get out don't dream about getting caught. Be realistic!"

The men were silent for a moment when I had finished, and then the schoolteacher made a comment. "It seems to me," he said, "that whether you know it or not, you've just come up with an idea that we might adopt as a permanent slogan. You're right of course about what we dream in here. I've found myself doing that. What it all boils down to is that we're not thinking realistically about what life is going to be like on the outside. So why not make that our motto? Think realistically."

The teacher's idea obviously appealed to several people. Charlie, Pegleg, and Wash Carver were nodding. Lefty Boyd said, "Sounds good to me."

"Okay," I said, "Let's put it to a vote."

The vote was unanimously in favor.

At the next Monday's class, Wash Carver got up and said: "We all agreed we were going to think realistically. Well, I've got a realistic question for you, Bill. How are we going to *stay* out of this joint when we can't *get* out?"

There was an immediate murmur of assent from the class. I knew what they were talking about. A man with a date for parole has to show the parole people a "plan," which means a schedule of where he's going to live and how, and, most important, where he's going to work and for whom. Parole boards will not release a man who has no way to support himself when he's out. They reason that a parolee with no honest livelihood is certain to resume his career in crime as soon as he needs money badly enough. Buck Rogers had given me a list of men whose parole dates were already past but who had to stay in Lansing because they had no job offers. We call such men "overdue."

Getting jobs for convicts is not easy. Unfortunately, the public demands that a man who is released from prison be employed, but at the same time potential employers usually regard ex-convicts with suspicion. In order for my program to succeed, I knew from the very beginning that I would have to acquaint some Kansas City businessmen with our work and, in so doing, show them at the same time that convicts were human beings.

With this in mind, I had asked Warden Crouse for permission to bring in outsiders, which he readily granted. The outsiders I chose were business and professional men I knew personally. During the past several weeks our class had been observed by the president of a construction company, the owner of a garage, a dentist, several lawyers, one banker, and other men in the business community.

This was a new thing at Lansing. Up to then there had seldom been any visitors allowed inside the main prison. This had been a help to me in getting businessmen to come, because there was lot of curiosity about what went on behind those grim walls. Although they thought they came only to watch and listen, several of them had already been persuaded to furnish jobs to our men. But they could not conceivably employ more than a very few of the men in the class, and most of the class was overdue. Wash Carver, who had raised the question, had a parole date that was nearly two years past, and there were others even worse off.

I said, "It's rough, Wash, but no rougher than it was before this program started. If you have to do flat time, that's bad. But when you get out, you can stay out."

But they weren't buying it. Do your time flat, and you still had to find a job, start stealing again, or starve to death.

Marble made the point, "You got out on the street in a big war, Bill, when the shipyards were hiring anybody. Now I sit in the cell every night and answer want ads. On prison paper, that's going to go out with a prison censor's stamp on it. The other night I figured I'd written three hundred letters, and my date was six months ago, and I haven't had one single answer. You think I can keep this up forever?"

I didn't think so. One-eyed Marble was a man, not an angel.

So I was out evenings and weekends, scouring Kansas City and Kansas in general for men who would offer jobs to the people in the class.

Buck Rogers' list showed a total of ninety-three men who were overdue. The state of Kansas was supporting them at a minimum cost of a hundred and fifty dollars a month per capita. Which means that the state was spending almost a hundred and fifty thousand dollars a year to keep men in prison *after* the board of paroles had ruled them safe to be on the streets.

I ended the class that night by promising the men that I would, somehow, figure out a way to alleviate that situation.

I'd opened my mouth and made another promise. Now I had to think up a way of keeping it. So I proposed to the parole board that the state hire an employment officer who would have the sole duty of finding jobs for overdue men. They could have hired a good man for about ten thousand a year, and perhaps maintaining an office would have cost them about as much. Twenty thousand dollars to save a hundred and fifty thousand dollars. The idea was turned down cold by the board, though the director of prisons endorsed it. This was not the first time we had trouble with the Kansas board of paroles, nor was it to be the last.

The trouble lay in nature of the appointments to the board of paroles, and this applies to many other states as well as to Kansas. A governor is usually not required to select men with any related experience for the board. Selections often go to friends and political supporters who know nothing about the job when appointed and seldom bother to study it while serving.

Parole must, to be effective, protect society. The best way to do this is to select men for parole who are, in fact, ready to be released because of a change in their thinking. But parole boards have little real insight into a man's thinking. Every convict knows exactly what to expect when he appears. First the board discusses the man's previous crimes in order to determine whether he has learned his lesson, as they call it. Then a member usually asks, "Are you going to behave yourself if we let you out?" What do they expect the man to say?

Serving on a parole board is no job for amateurs or political hacks. A parole board should number among its members a psychiatrist skilled in the use of Sodium Pentothal, a knowledgeable and modern penologist, a polygraph operator, and one ex-convict. Unfortunately, this is not the kind of board I brought my proposal to.

They rejected my proposal simply because it was new. They were sold on the belief that a non-rocked boat sails best. But sailing is not very lively when the anchor is dragging.

I opened the next meeting by telling the men what I had tried to do about helping them to get jobs and how I had failed. I assured them I'd keep working on it, and then we went on to the regular business of the class.

"So far," I said, "the best thing that happened in this class was when we adopted a slogan and started examining our thoughts in the light of whether or not we're being realistic. I think the time has come for us to go further. We need a set of guidelines to help us in our thinking. Some sort of steps that we can follow in a logical progression to help us make this change we're always talking about. But I don't want to set down the steps for you to follow. I want you to do that yourselves. Any ideas?"

The class was full of suggestions and the rest of the session passed quickly but without anything really being settled. At the end I said, "All right, our time is up for tonight and we haven't accomplished much. I'll give you an assignment for next week's class. Each of you write down whatever steps you think are most important in helping a man change his thinking. Bring them to me next week and we'll discuss them one by one."

The slips that were turned in the next week varied from handwritten scrawls to lavishly decorated and laboriously printed documents. The men had spent a lot of time working on them—they had plenty of time.

I read the suggestion aloud, and as soon as I had finished there was a clamor. Everybody wanted to talk at once.

So, in order to get them really thinking, I asked the first-time losers to put their hands up. Only two showed. When I asked for two-time losers, about half the men put a hand up. The rest—almost a half—had fallen three times or more.

Then I asked how many of them were in for sex crimes. No one wanted to show, but I cajoled a few hands into the air. Then I ran through all the other categories, from pickpocket to armed robbery and murder, and finally I was able to say what I had hoped to say. "All right. What we have here is a typical cross section of every prison in the country. And that means the rules we draw up could be used in every one of those prisons. And someday, perhaps, they will be. That's something to think about."

That quieted them down. They felt important. For some of them I am sure it was almost the first time in their lives that they had had that feeling without doing something violent.

"For that reason, you are going to have to agree—unanimously on every rule and every word in every rule that we set down."

Several nodded. All were very serious.

One of the men got up and went to the blackboard—as I remember it, he was a handsome young bank robber with the memorable name of Leon Sessions Emory. I spread a piece of paper in front of me on the desk, and we started. We had been hammering at that word "change" for so long that about half the slips had used it.

The first step, exactly as it stands today, was written there in forty seconds.

*Facing the truth about ourselves and the world
around us, we decided we needed to change.*

Getting a step in forty seconds was so encouraging that I thought we might have our guidelines that night.

But the second step took us the rest of the two hours. It was:

*Realizing that there is a power from which we can
gain strength, we have decided to use that power.*

At first the word "force" crept in and was voted down almost at once. Force was what kept them in prison, force was for the captain of the Yard and his bulls. Anything about God, or the Lord, or the Almighty was out. Prisons are full of agnostics. Of course there are some sincerely religious men in any prison, but it's also true that, for many of the cons who claim to have been "saved" while doing time, religion is a shuck. There are exceptions even to this. One such man, Phil Thatcher, was a hard-core Main Yard convict in one of the toughest prisons in the country. When he was saved, he got it so deeply he went to the warden and confessed to a long string of crimes he had never even been suspected of. But when the authorities asked him who his confederates had been—and he had never committed a crime alone—he said, "Jesus made me a man, not a stool pigeon." So he remained in prison and preached there, and the men respected his solidity, but they couldn't buy religion, even from him. I don't know why. Maybe they felt that if there was an Almighty, he wouldn't have created the world they resent so much.

After God, force, and other unacceptable words had been vetoed, "power" began to be heard more and more. The power of positive thinking, the power of a group working together, the power of the subconscious mind. As I have said, there were some educated men there.

The next week we put those two rules back on the board, and in two hours of hard, sweaty work, we added two more. They were:

Evaluating ourselves by taking an honest self-appraisal, we examined both our strengths and our weaknesses.

Endeavoring to help ourselves overcome our weaknesses, we enlisted the aid of that power to help us concentrate on our strengths.

The third week we got one more.

Observing that daily progress is necessary, we set an attainable goal toward which we can work each day.

Then the fourth week, we added a sixth step, but with trouble.

Leon kept erasing and writing in until the blackboard was a mess.

The sixth step read:

Maintaining our own freedom, we pledge ourselves to help others as we have been helped.

And at that stage we thought we were through. We had six good rules to guide any man who wanted to change from a recidivist to a man free for life. But then someone proposed another, and we realized it was as important as anything we had formulated up to then.

It read:

Deciding that our freedom is worth more than our resentments, we are using that power to help free us from those resentments.

At first we couldn't decide where it belonged. After the second step? At the end? In the middle? Leon kept erasing and writing, squeezing lines in between lines and then lines between those. I could barely read the crossed out, rewritten, scribbled-on paper on my desk. Finally we decided that the new rule was the fifth.

The two hours were nearly over. Then something happened that I have never been certain I understand. Pegleg put up his hand, his bald head gleaming. I pointed at him. He said, "Bill, read the first word of each rule."

I did: "Facing, realizing, evaluating, endeavoring, deciding, observing, maintaining. What are you are getting at, Peg?"

He said, "The first letter of each word spells FREEDOM."

I've never been sure myself whether this happened by accident or not. Leon couldn't have done it—he was putting the steps down as the class dictated.

I couldn't have done it. I never touched the board, and I only told Leon to write them down as the class unanimously agreed on the proper wording and position. I do not understand how it happened—all I know is what I have told here.

Chapter 4

As the men became more involved with the class, the tone of the individual interviews changed, and some of the men at least were finally beginning to give some thought to the individual problems they might face when they got out. But they were still more willing to talk about one another than about themselves.

The most discouraging thing about all the loose talk, the whines and the complaints, was that it showed me I wasn't really reaching the hard-core convict. He would know better than to talk that much.

From my point of view, this was very important. The toughest of the convicts in the prison, the incorrigibles, the Main Yard leaders, were exactly the ones I wanted to draw into the prerelease class. They were the ones who had the best chance of sticking to a resolution once they had made it, because the same strength they devoted to being incorrigible could also be

used to keep them straight. And besides, the whole population looked up to them. If they bought what I was selling, the
others would follow along naturally. But I needed at least one
Main Yard leader and I didn't have one.

Then Karl Bowen came into the office. A small guy, but
tough all the way through, Karl is half-German and half-
Cherokee; and the combination has turned out a brooding man.

He sat down, his eyes glowing with a somber light that I
was to get to know well.

"What's your game, Sands?"

"Bill. I don't like to be called by my last name."

He shrugged.

"I'm asking you what your game is? What's with you?" he
repeated.

"Come to the Monday night class and find out."

"I know what goes on in the class," he said. "I asked the
guys who go to it. I don't buy what you claim to be selling."

"Then what did you come in here for?"

"Because I heard that you shut off the guys who talk too
much about things that aren't your business. So I got curious.
I thought I'd have a look at you."

Right then I knew this was the man I'd been looking for—
the first hard-core convict to come to see me. If I could sell
him . . .

But I'd never had a tougher prospect. Just looking at Karl
told me that. I've had enough resentments of my own to recognize the feeling, and his resentment stood out all over him.

"Okay," I said. "Come to the classes and get a good look.
What's your time worth?"

The faintest glow of humor showed up on Karl's rocky,
swarthy face.

"Quite a bit to the state," he said. "At least they went to some trouble bringing me back from an escape to make sure I serve all of it."

"Big deal. That's what they do with most guys who escape. Now what about the class? Are you curious enough to take a good look?"

He stood up.

"Okay. I'll come to the class. But I'm telling you again, I'm not buying." He walked to the door, paused, added "Bill." Then he went out.

After that I started digging into Karl's story. I needed to know what was in his official prison record—what we call his jacket. He was classed as "incorrigible." Besides his escape, he had many prior convictions on his rap sheet. He had no respect for the law no hope for himself. He had been brutalized by the kind of treatment he'd found in prison.

Karl's escape sounds like an oldtime comedy. On the screen, you'd expect Laurel and Hardy to be playing it. But his story is important. It stamps him: solid con.

Somehow Karl's date of release from Lansing got transposed in the official records that are kept in the prison office. So he was called from his cell, handed a suit of civilian clothes and twenty dollars, and "dressed out" the front gate, as a discharge. A straight-time discharge, that is, which means that he didn't even have to answer to a parole board.

Karl kept his mouth shut. Wouldn't you? He beat it across the river into Missouri, and by the time the mistake had been discovered he was three hundred miles into Missouri and settled down. It was no small mistake, either. He still had seven to go. Seven years—not days or months.

Whether he could be legally returned to Lansing was never determined. The warden and his staff didn't feel like having the attorney general of Kansas send a lawyer into a Missouri court to ask for extradition. They didn't need publicity that badly.

What they decided to do about the matter is unbelievable.

They sent a guard—a single, solitary, unhappy guard—into Missouri to bring him back. The guard was armed with chains, manacles, leg irons, a gun, and a badge that was absolutely worthless the minute he crossed the Missouri River.

To add to this idiocy, they picked a guard who had just come off the night shift and gave him a ticket on a day coach. It took him all day to rattle across the state to the town where Karl was living. And when he arrived he was completely worn out. It's likely that the errand he was doing made him too nervous to get much sleep on the grimy plush of a noisy smoker. But his gun wasn't tired. When he walked up and drew his gun, Karl decided to allow himself to be shackled and pushed on a train back to Kansas City.

The guard manacled Karl to the armrest of the inside seat of a day coach and prepared to get some rest. All the passengers in the car could see what was going on. It must have brightened the prospect of a dreary trip for them.

The minute the guard's eyes closed, Karl went into his act. He rattled his chains till his keeper woke up again. "I gotta go to the men's room," Karl said. He added quickly: "I just can't help it."

When a Kansas yard bull dresses a prisoner to travel, he does a thorough job of it. Karl would have fetched a nice sum in a junkyard. He had a chain around his waist with handcuffs fastened to it. Then another chain ran from the first one down to his ankles, where it was attached to heavy shackles. All this was standard for any Kansas prisoner en route. Karl's man had added a chain that wound around the prisoner's neck and ran down to join the iron waist-belt.

Remember, Karl is not very big and he must have looked the most forlorn sight in Missouri as he hobbled up the aisle past all the passengers. At least he remembers that several of them clucked sympathetically.

The guard, of course, followed him to the little compartment, waited outside, and then herded Karl back down the aisle again. The guard's gun by now must have looked as big as all of Karl, who was bent over as though he could barely carry the iron. He was making himself look as small as possible. Karl never misses a bet.

Nearly back to his seat, he added sound to his performance. Clanking the chains, he raised his voice: "Gee, Mr. Guard, this stuff is on awful tight. It's cutting into me."

"Shut up," the guard said. "I'll decide whether you hurt or not."

The clucks got louder and spread a little among Karl's audience.

So they settled down again, with Karl fastened to the armrest and the guard trying to sleep on his half of the seat. Karl gave him fifteen minutes. Then he woke him. "I gotta go again. Sorry, but after all, it was you guys beat up on my kidneys. I haven't been right since."

What could the guard do? I'm no screw-lover, but the first time I heard Karl tell the story, I almost felt sorry for that man.

Karl ran him three times in all. Then the guard blew up. "Look, damn it, control yourself for a while. I'm not being paid to run you up and down the aisle all day. Just sit there and let your kidneys bust!"

Karl said, "Yes, sir."

The audience, no doubt, got ready to write their congress-men.

This time Karl didn't stir. He sat there, crouched over, looking like a small, inoffensive man who'd be beaten if he let his hardware make even a small rattle.

The guard fell asleep. He fell deeper and deeper asleep as Karl left him alone. Thirty minutes after the last "kidney attack" the guard was snoring gently.

Fine. But Karl could move only about half a foot away from his waist chain. It was enough for a patient man. First he worked the chain around until his hand was only six inches from the guard's pocket. Then he slowly leaned his small body over until he was almost on top of his keeper.

Then he had the key.

Karl was too busy to watch his audience, but they must have been holding their breath. In any event, none of them yelled copper. Karl went through all the complicated business of taking the chains, the manacles, and the shackles off himself and putting them on the guard without interruption.

Then Karl Bowen stood up and made a speech. "I haven't taken this man's gun, and I haven't taken his money," he told the gaping carload. "I hate to leave anyone in his spot, but you folks can see how it is."

He says that he thinks some of the passengers would have applauded if they hadn't been afraid of waking the sleeping beauty.

The train was going about forty miles an hour, much too fast for safe jumping, but Karl had very little choice. If he waited for a slowdown, the guard could wake up, or one of the passengers could start reconsidering what his civic duty was. So he jumped and hit the embankment with enough force to roll him back toward the track. He didn't go under the train, but he snapped a bone in his ankle against a switch stand.

So he walked to the nearest highway on a broken ankle.

Nothing that had happened had improved his appearance. It was quite a while before a car stopped for him. The man driving it watched critically as Karl climbed clumsily in. The ankle, of course, was badly swollen by now—just getting into a car was a terrible job.

"Where you going?"

"Kansas City, sir."

"Okay, I'm going that far. You don't look so hot. What happened?"

If you ring a bell every time you feed a dog, sooner or later his mouth will start watering at the sound of the bell without the sight or smell of food. Karl was conditioned thoroughly. Now his own private bell rang, and it tolled "The Law," without the sight of a badge or a gun.

The reaction is automatic. Talk soft, but not scared. Talk fast, but not too fast. Karl is an expert, a post-graduate. "Sir, I've been working up in Springfield, Illinois. In a grocery store." Who is more of a squarejohn than a grocery clerk? "But my mom wrote me she wanted me near her. She's getting along, sir, and I'm her youngest. She says she's lined up a job for me with a cousin of hers. He's got a little grocery store, too."

All he got for this was a grunt. "I just hated to tell Mom how little I'd been making, and that I hadn't been able to save a single penny," he went on, sincerity dripping from him like beer from a broken tap. "So I decided I'd try and ride the rods home, you know, under a railroad car like you see on TV. Mister, never try it, and you better believe me. It's rough under there. When the train slowed down a little, I just bailed out. I know it's not safe to hitchhike, but anything was better than what I was taking under that car."

The driver laughed a little. "You're safe enough with me," he said. "I'm a deputy sheriff."

Is that news? Karl asked himself.

"I'm on my way to Kansas City to pick up a man to return him to jail in my county." The law shook its noble head. "It's a good thing you were over the county line when I picked you up, or I'd have to hold you for trial, too. It's against the law to stow away on a train."

"I didn't know that, sir. I wasn't doing anyone any harm but myself."

"Why, you were trying to cheat the railroad out of your fare."

"I never thought of it that way, sir."

"Yep. But I guess you've learned your lesson."

Karl said he certainly had.

The majesty of the law forgave him. "That rattler you were on is the four-o-two out of my town," the deputy said. "It stops all along the line, picking up the evening mail. I'll get you to the Kansas City depot before the train gets there, and you can walk out like a law-abiding, ticket-buying citizen. Your mother going to meet you?"

"Oh no, sir, she's not well enough. My cousin will be there, though."

"Well, he'll never know a thing, if you can figure out something to tell him about your clothes. And your ankle. How does it feel now?"

"Much better," Karl said, "and so do I. You've sure said a lot to straighten me out, sir." You can't put it on too strong with a small-town cop.

The deputy let him off at the railroad station in Kansas City—Missouri, of course. Karl wasn't going to cross into Kansas.

A sensible man would have beat it away from there as soon as the car was out of sight. But Karl—like a lot of good guys—has more guts than sense. He waited around to see what happened when the train came in carrying one Kansas screw, firmly anchored to an armrest.

It was sort of disappointing, he always said afterward. The train came in, and in a few minutes a work crew hurried down to the tracks, carrying wrenches and a blowtorch. All too soon the guard came out, with only a small piece of armrest fastened to him. Karl had hoped he'd have to take the whole chair back to Lansing, maybe the whole car.

What happened next is not very funny.

Karl went back to St. Joseph, Missouri, with an elastic bandage on his ankle, and settled down again.

But the government of the sovereign state of Kansas didn't settle down at all. Now the prison officials knew they couldn't keep their goofup to themselves. They had to take the Department of Corrections at Topeka in on the story, and the department had to ask the advice of the attorney general. The opinion of his office wasn't very favorable to the warden and his men. They couldn't charge Karl with escaping the first time, because they had turned him out themselves, and they couldn't charge him with escaping from the train, because every man has the right to defend himself from a felony against his person, i.e., kidnapping.

They could of course ask the governor of Kansas to ask the governor of Missouri for extradition. But there was no way to do that without spreading the whole story across the pages of the Kansas City *Star*, and probably all the rest of the newspapers in the country, too.

So they appealed to Karl's mother—who, incidentally, was hardly the doddering Mom of the tale Karl told the deputy sheriff.

Finally a meeting was arranged in the warden's office at Lansing. The governor sent a pardon and parole attorney as his personal representative, empowered to talk for the governor himself. The warden was there, of course, and Karl was represented by his lawyer and his mother.

The lawyers dickered and made offers and counter-offers. That's what attorneys are for. They got closer and closer together, and finally they reached an agreement. Karl was to return and give himself up, then he was to serve one calendar year out of the seven he still owed Kansas. After that the governor's man guaranteed that the governor would issue a decree of executive clemency, and Karl would go free.

It wasn't a bad offer. That seven years was a heavy cloud hanging over Karl's head.

So twenty-four hours after the conference broke up, Karl walked back into Lansing. The prisoners, of course, greeted him with joy and admiration. He'd made a fool out of the screws who kept them in misery. When they learned that he had conned a deputy into helping him in his getaway, it seemed as if Christmas had come twice that year.

The guards and their officers weren't so cordial. The first thing they wanted Karl to do was to sign a complaint against the guard who had kidnapped him. That they could handle quietly.

Karl refused. Even if the man was a screw, Karl was not a stool pigeon.

A lieutenant of the Yard had been dressing Karl in. He said, "You'll sign or you'll go to the hole."

"That wasn't in the deal," Karl said.

"To hell with the deal," the lieutenant said. "Show me where it says how you're going to serve your year. I wouldn't have made a deal with you, and neither would the captain. Him and me are going to make you wish to God you'd serve the whole seven like any other inmate, instead of doing one straight in segregation."

Segregation is the official word for solitary—the convicts call it jail. In Lansing at that time it was located in a separate building in the middle of the prison. It consisted of a row of damp, unheated cells with solid steel doors and no window. Once the doors were closed there was practically no light at all.

Karl was stripped naked before being thrown into his dungeon. At night he was issued a couple of blankets to keep off pneumonia. He had no pallet or bed of any sort. The cell was provided with two buckets, one for a toilet and one to hold drinking water.

That was his home, and his food was carrots and cabbage. A man can live on that, and Karl did. There was some variety to his life. Once a week the lieutenant of the Yard tear-gassed the cell.

Finally the yard captain, second in command of the whole prison, came into Karl's cell. His appearance was an improvement on being tear-gassed—but not much. He wasn't there to see if Karl Bowen was happy and comfortable. He offered to let him out if he would testify against the guard who had gone to sleep on the train.

"Do your own dirty business your own dirty way," Karl said. "I wouldn't lift a finger to push anybody into your hands.

You ever notice anything? When a deal is made with a con, it's the other guy—guard, warden, captain, squarejohn—who breaks his word. It's not the con. You guys got the upper hand, but we're better than you at that."

"That little speech will cost you another thirty days here."

"Come back in thirty days and I'll have a better one for you."

Eventually they turned him out into the main prison, almost dead, but still fighting. A tough man, with nothing left inside him but resentment and cold hatred of the guards, the captain, the lieutenant, the warden, and the whole system—politicians, taxpayers, civil servants—that backed up the prison officials, that paid their salaries.

Do you expect a man who had been through all that to be logical? Do you think you would come out of there sane—let alone reasonable, logical, with good, cool judgment?

Karl's troubles were far from over. They had hardly started. The sovereign state of Kansas was just warming up. The year Karl had agreed to spend in Lansing passed, but nobody handed Karl his suit and his walk-away money. He just went on serving time, in daylong pieces.

Finally he told his cell mate, "I guess I better try and see the warden."

The captain and the guards probably would have kept Karl out of the warden's office if they had been able to, but a second convict knows the ropes. He got to the warden about a week after he started trying.

Karl faced the warden, and the warden obviously wasn't happy when he saw Karl. A lesser man would have pushed the job off on a subordinate. "Bad news, Karl," he said at once. "The governor's going out of office, and I don't think he's going to sign your commutation paper. It's been sitting on his desk since before your time came up. Karl, if he hasn't signed by now, I don't think he will."

Karl blew up. "Why the hell not? He made a deal."

The warden looked down at his hands. "I know. But I guess he doesn't want to embarrass his administration or the new one by turning you out."

Karl sort of shrank into himself. He couldn't even answer.

The warden said, "You have every right to be angry. If it were up to me, I'd turn you out."

Karl swallowed. "Yeah," he said, "I guess you would. You're not lousy enough to be governor of this lousy state. Warden, you got one thing wrong."

The warden looked up and met Karl's eyes. "Yes, Karl?"

"I'm not mad, warden. You got that wrong. I'm just smarter than I was. I just learned never to trust anybody, any kind of a squarejohn, in or out of a guard's uniform. You got a bad con on your hands, warden. If you think I was hard before wait around and see me now. And you aren't going to be able to break me. Not you—not your guards—not your ape captain or his meatball lieutenants—not your jail—and not your tear gas, either."

And Karl turned and walked out of the office to be taken back into the joint by the waiting guards, who had surely heard every word.

That had been three years before Karl and I talked in Chaplain Post's little office.

After our talk Karl kept his word. He came to every Monday night class. He never said anything, just sat there taking it all in.

Then I said I wanted to see him in the office again. He showed up, looking as impassive as if he were all Indian, instead of just half. I said:

"How long have you been coming to our classes, Karl?"

"Three months."

"Then nothing I say now is going to be very new to you. Or very convincing."

The impassive face didn't change.

"If you mean I still don't buy what you're selling, you're right."

"All we're selling is freedom."

"The price is too damned high," said Karl.

"Why?"

"Bill, I like you and I think you're solid, but, boy, you've been out too long. You got it made on the outside."

Made, indeed! Since I'd taken on the program, all I had to show for my life was bills and debts. Our comfortable home had gone by now, and so had a lot of other things. The object I called my car was a wreck I'd picked up for a song, and we were now living in a drab little house we didn't own.

There wasn't any use telling Karl about all that. Not in his present mood, anyway.

So all I said was: "It's because I do remember that I stay out, Karl. Do me a favor?"

No answer to that one. But the glowing eyes watched me carefully.

So I went on, "Let's you and me have a debate before the class. I'll try to show where you're wrong and you try to show where I'm wrong. Fair?"

"Sure. It'll be lively anyway."

Monday night, when the class met, Karl showed up, still glowering, still silent, every line of his weathered face saying he wasn't buying anything from me or anybody else. Still, it was nice he was there. The time I had to stand up and talk would be shortened, and the class's interest would be freshened.

As I started, Karl Bowen regarded me calmly. He was expecting a good show, his face said, but that was all it meant to him—a break in the monotony. I wanted him mad before he got on his feet. I said: "One of the guys in this class came to me the other day and said he wasn't buying a thing we're selling here."

Not a quiver on Karl's face.

"I'm talking about Karl Bowen. I don't think he's stupid, so it must be that he likes guards and stool pigeons and punks."

That got him. He came to his feet, eyes flashing and blood pumping to make his high cheekbones look more Indian than ever.

He is not the shouting kind, but the restrained anger in his voice made him sound as if he were shouting. "Wait a minute, Bill! I never said I liked screws and stool pigeons, and you damn well know it!"

I snapped back at him, but my anger was calculated. "Didn't you say the only thing you wanted was to get even, no matter what it cost you? Didn't you say you were going to make 'them' sorry for the months of carrots and cabbage and tear gas?"

He nodded slowly, puzzled. "Yeah. Yeah, I said all that. And I stand by it."

"Then you admit you like this joint, its screws and its stool pigeons."

Karl was quiet and he shook his head. "You're not making any sense," he said finally.

"No? You'll be out of here soon. But a little while after that—days, weeks, maybe months—you'll be back. And you know that except for a few faces nothing will have changed. There'll be still ape guards and punks and stool pigeons, lousy food, and gray walls around the Yard, and the hole always waiting with a fresh supply of cabbage and carrots—and tear gas."

His face was dark red now.

Karl asked, "What the hell right have you to tell me I'm coming back here?"

"Here or some other place. Any man who goes out of here with resentments choking him up to the tonsils is coming back. Because resentment calls for violence, and violence calls for breaking the law and back you go."

Karl just shook his head.

I said, "You have your choice, Karl. Come back—or give up your resentments."

He took plenty of time to answer. He was giving up the hard way, which was the way Karl had done everything, all his life.

"How can I?" he asked. "These guys have kicked me around for years, on a doublecross from the governor himself. How can I quit without trying to even the score?"

I had one argument left.

"What you call getting even, Karl, is just hurting yourself. When you go out, the captain will still be in here with the screws, the punks, the stool pigeons, and the stink of mess-hall food and bodies and floor sweepings. And if you and a few thousand like you can stay out, the captain and his screws will be out of work. Can you imagine the captain digging a ditch, which is the only other job he can get?"

The class began to laugh. Even Karl smiled a little. The captain of the yard hadn't lifted anything heavier than a club in thirty years. He had a paunch like Santa Claus's, but he didn't go "Ho, ho, ho."

"So get out, Karl, and stay out. And every so often send the captain a picture of yourself dressed in a sharp suit. Maybe have it taken in a Playboy Club, with you surrounded by bunnies. Just write on the other side, 'Dear Captain, Here I am with all the pretty girls. How come you're in there with the queens and punks? You must like it for some reason, huh?' "

The class burst into laughter. Then, one by one, they stopped and waited for Karl to answer me.

Slowly he smiled.

"Bill, that's a hell of a good idea." Then his hard suspicious face closed up again. "I'll think it over. Let you know when I've made up my mind."

And he sat down again.

It was the best I could hope for. Karl wouldn't decide anything on an impulse. But if his thinking it over ended the way I hoped, I knew he'd stick.

Chapter 5

I was dead broke. Friends I had made in Kansas City lent me money, assuring me that I would be rich when the book I had written about my life was published. Rue Holland was particularly generous—he was in the construction business with his father and brothers, all of whom became close friends of mine. Dr. C. Leslie Thompson and his wife Barbara were other wholehearted friends to the program and to me. But I wasn't accustomed to living on handouts, and as time went on I found it harder and harder to fight down my feelings of humiliation and irritation.

I wasn't lifting a finger to get out of this situation, but by pure chance I almost did get out of it before I had any results to show for my months of work. I thought of giving up only because, out of a clear sky, an insurance company offered me a job with a guaranteed income of twenty thousand dollars a year and a strong probability of making more than that almost at once. The Hollands, the Thompsons, and other friends had been wonderful about the money I owned them, and Pony and Bonnie were unfailingly cheerful about the skimping I was imposing on them. But did I have the right to turn down this windfall, with no certainty that the work I was doing at Lansing would ever be worth anything to anyone? I didn't know. I do know I was sorely tempted. I went through a Friday and a Saturday night with no sleep at all.

As I have said, I'm not a religious man. Maybe I would be one if all ministers were like Jim Post. Or maybe I just admired Jim as a man. At any rate, non-churchgoing Bill Sands took his troubles to the chaplain on Sunday afternoon.

Most modern ministers look like anything but the traditional black-clad person. Jim carries his unclerical dressing a little further than most—this Sunday he had on a hound's-tooth brown sports coat, a suede vest with brass buttons, and light gray slacks. The clothes set off his big form, and his little mustache added a sporty touch.

As we passed through the living room, I saw Mrs. Post—a professional decorator who has given their house a warm look with colonial antiques and reproductions—working at her art. She was arranging and rearranging some dried flowers. They looked fine to me the first time, but she kept doing them over.

Jim asked me if I had troubles.

"Morals and responsibilities," I said. I tried to keep my tone light, but of course that was impossible.

"Those fall into a minister's department, all right," he answered seriously.

"I'm really here not because you're a minister, but because you more than anybody else got me started out at Lansing. That gives you the right to be the first to hear this. Jim, I don't see how I can go on with the class. I owe everybody in Kansas City, Kansas, and most of the people in Kansas City, Missouri, and I just can't go on deadbeating merchants and taking loans from friends. I think it's time to go to work and earn some money."

"Anything in particular lead to this?"

"Yes and no. It's been coming on a long time."

I told him about the loans from the Thompsons and Rue Holland.

After a moment's hesitation Jim said, "Bill, your friends are decent people who want to do some real good in the world. If they contributed to an organized charity, they would expect the charity to have paid workers, wouldn't they?"

"But that's exactly what I'm not!"

"No. In this case the donors will get their money back. That's on the plus side, not the minus."

"You're very convincing," I admitted. "But there's Pony and our daughter Bonnie. We're really only just getting by, and it isn't fair to them."

The chaplain nodded slowly.

"Yes. A man owes something to his family. A good deal. But how long is it going to be before the Lansing movement is on its feet? Three months, six months? Pony and Bonnie have a right to be proud of you too, and when this thing succeeds—when, not if—they'll have a man they can really look up to. You've hung on this long, don't give up now. And there is always your book to look forward to. It may pay off everything."

"And it may not," I said. "But something has changed, besides my debts to Holland and the Thompsons. I've been offered a job that would pay about four hundred a week. What do you think my creditors would say if they knew I turned it down? What would you say if I owed you—oh—say a thousand dollars, and passed up a chance to pay it back?"

"You know very well what I'd say, Bill."

His quiet voice brought me up short. I said, "Sorry, Jim. Yes, I do. I didn't mean you personally."

He waved away the apologies. He said, "I don't know how many people you owe money to. But there are about a hundred men in that class out at the penitentiary. Are you going to get up in front of them and say, 'Sorry boys. No more help inside, no jobs when you get out. I've got to make mine with a big salary.'"

"That's hitting below the belt, Jim!"

He stood up. If he'd heard me, he didn't show it. "The men need to know what you've learned in your twenty years of staying out. They need the help you'll give them in the jobs you'll find them." He emphasized the word "you" every time he said it. "There's no one else doing all that, there's no one else available to do it."

It sounded better when someone else said it than it had when I said it to myself. But . . .

"You've heard the old saying, Jim? 'Fire all essential and irreplaceable men.'"

"Every rule has its exception." He walked up and down the room a couple of times, and then sat down again. "We're quibbling. The point is, you can't fight destiny. I honestly believe God meant for you to do what you're doing, and that this path you're treading is inexorably the path you have to tread."

"Come off it, Jim. Lay off the God bit. Don't preach to me."

He could have said that if I didn't want preaching I shouldn't have called on a minister on Sunday. He didn't, and I didn't think of it till much later. He didn't say anything, just left it up to me.

I turned over what he had said. Finally I said, "You say that this is my life's work, but how can I *know* it is?"

Jim's gaze was steady on my face. "There is no hard and fast rule that I know of." He rubbed his temples. "I can give you my concept. To me, life is like an oriental rug, and we're like little bugs crawling across it. First, we're right in a forest of black, then one of red, then one of blue, and in each forest the whole world looks black or red or blue. But if we could be suspended a couple of feet above the rug, on a totally different plane, we'd be able to see and understand what the colors mean, where they fit into the great and beautiful pattern."

"I'm not trying to be irreverent, chaplain, but what you're saying is, only God knows if this is my life's work. Right?"

He smiled. "I wouldn't put it that bluntly. I believe that man is created in God's image, and he is the only creature on earth who can think in three dimensions—past, present, and future. Which enables us to draw comparisons, and on the basis of those, to choose our own course of action. Each man for himself."

Without knowing it, he had almost phrased the solid con's core of philosophy. Each man does his own time. It cut pretty close to me. I asked, "But how do we know if we've made the right choice?" This time he grinned openly. "Easy, Bill. The Creator gave us a little something called a conscience. All you have to do is follow its dictates, and the way is made clear and smooth."

When I was a prizefighter, I could usually tell when the judges had marked me the loser of a round. I had that feeling now.

We sat there a few minutes in silence. I guess the chaplain would call it meditation. Then I said, "O.K., Jim, I got the message. But the irreplaceable-man theory still holds. I could drop dead. I was almost in a bad auto accident on my way out to the joint Friday. Dig me up a man to split the load with."

"What kind of a man?"

"You know. A guy like me, an ex-con who's stayed out and wants to help other men stay out. You've got the contacts. See what you can do."

"Fine. I'll get right on it."

Back home, all Pony asked me was, "Going to stick with it, Bill?"

When I nodded, she grinned. But later, when I was just dozing off, she asked me what Jim had said. I mumbled, "Something about bugs in a rug," and went to sleep, leaving her to wonder if she had married a maniac.

I went on with the prerelease class and redoubled my efforts to help the overdue men get jobs. I made speeches before service clubs and luncheon groups and organizations interested in convicts, in the hope of finding potential employers. This meant missing an occasional Monday night class. When that happened, Jim Emerson held down the moderator's platform at the prison.

Gradually I became aware that on the nights he led the class, things didn't go so well. I couldn't understand why. Jim was never a convict, but he was working heart and soul for the program, and the men knew it and respected him for it. They didn't identify with him as they did with me, but I was sure they weren't hostile either.

Squarejohn or not, Jim subscribed to the convict code. Ride your own beef, and don't be a stool pigeon. So he didn't say anything to me until things got so bad that at last he told me that he didn't want to take any more classes, because they were hard on him and weren't doing the men any good. I figured someone must have been giving him a bad time, so I nosed around and found out who it was and what he was doing.

He was a big, powerful man who liked to be called Hardrock. Every time Jim tried to teach something, Hardrock would argue with him, not constructively but in bullying contradiction of everything Jim said. The other cons were letting Hardrock say what he liked, not because they agreed with him, but because they thought that everyone ought to ride his own beef. Mistakenly, they thought that this beef wasn't theirs. Jim just couldn't handle the situation. It would take another convict to do so.

I wouldn't say that Hardrock was a Main Yard leader, but he certainly wanted to be one. He used his muscle to terrorize weaker men, but so far he hadn't dared take on anyone really tough. You need more than muscle to tackle a con like Karl Bowen, for instance, who has brains and guts if not size.

So Hardrock was looking for a way to make a reputation, and when I came along, he figured I just might be the way. Sniping at Jim Emerson was easier than confronting me, but the trouble he had been giving Jim was a kind of dress rehearsal. I was going to be the real target, and we both knew it. So did the men in the class. I knew I would have to face him down sooner or later—or stop coming to Lansing.

The prospect of a showdown wasn't pleasing. I had worked so hard getting the men to identify with me that, they no longer looked on me as a visitor, but as another convict. Which meant that if Hardrock wanted a reputation badly enough, he might try to kill me simply to prove he could do it. At Lansing men had been killed for less.

The fact that Jim Emerson could no longer take the class made it even more urgent that the chaplain find someone to help me. When I arrived at the prison the next morning, I was told that Jim Post wanted to see me in the officers' dining room, and I hoped it would be because he had come up with a guy to share the load.

In the officers' dining room a couple of convicts were mopping up the floor, of course. (I say "of course," because prison floors are constantly being mopped whether they need it or not. Since the early years of the twentieth century, it has been known that prisoners must work or they will deteriorate, sulk, and make trouble. But most productive work competes with private industry, illegally, so floors are mopped, walls are scrubbed, and the men get some exercise and a feeling of futility. As a result of all this labor, most joints smell of disinfectant, floor wax, and soap. It should be a cheerful smell and perhaps it is to visitors—but not to anyone who has ever done time.)

Chaplain Post was beaming happily, so I knew he had a surprise for me. Hopefully I told myself that he had found an ex-con who could collaborate with me at Lansing. I was aware that a number of ex-convicts keep in touch with their former chaplain, and though Jim frequently complained that the number was disappointingly small, a handful was better than none.

When we entered the officers' dining room, I saw a civilian drinking coffee, and after we had picked up our own cups, Jim introduced us. The new man's name was Ted. He was about thirty, of medium height and thin. The metal-rimmed glasses on his nose were the liveliest part of his face. As he extended a limp hand we told each other we were glad to meet. Then all three of us sat down and Post explained that Ted was an ex-prisoner.

"Ted has been out for five years," he went on, "and we have kept in touch with each other more or less steadily. He says he wants to help."

"I certainly do," put in Ted in a thin, high-pitched voice. "I've heard all about you on the radio, Mr. Sands, and read about you in the papers, too."

"Ted's a theological student," Jim said.

"You mean he's going to be a minister?" I asked.

"I certainly hope to be," Ted said.

It was at best only barely possible that any minister, ex-con or no, would be all right. It was not even remotely possible that Ted would be all right. The men would knock him around like a pingpong ball, and when the game was over, they would never come back to class.

I wasn't sure what to do. It was an awkward spot. Jim Post was obviously expecting that Ted would be right for the job, and I didn't want to disappoint him or hurt his feelings. At the same time I knew that I would not use Ted for as much as one class. Half stalling for time, I asked him, "What were you busted for?"

He turned red and looked at Jim for help.

"Does it matter?" asked the chaplain.

"Jim, you have been around convicts for years. You know they look up to some kinds of men and look down on others. Sure it matters."

And so saying, I turned my gaze back to Ted, who blushed still more deeply, and muttered, "A sex crime."

One of the moppers started mopping much faster, the other turned so that we could not see his face. I knew what they were thinking. Even pickpockets look down on rapos.

Not every man convicted of a sex crime suffers this contempt. I've known a few of the exceptions. I knew one man in San Quentin who was doing a sentence for rape under the following circumstances. He had been caught in a police raid on a house of prostitution. The prostitute with whom he was involved was only sixteen years old. He was charged, found guilty, and sent to prison for the crime of statutory rape. The girl's mother was the madam of the house and had served several jail sentences for prostitution. The girl herself had twice served time in the county jail on the same charge. The judge who had sentenced both mother and daughter as prostitutes was also the judge who sentenced the girl's customer to San Quentin! This convict had done a couple of long years in prison before he succeeded in bringing his case to the attention of the California authorities. Ultimately he was pardoned, but there was no way to refund the two years he'd served.

But the general run of the jute-mill rapo is a weak man, convicted of a crime of weakness. There is nothing such a man could do for one of my Seventh Step classes.

I would have been glad to stop there, but because of the two mop-pushers I had to get into the grapevine the news that I was not going to ask the men to listen to an ex-rapo do-gooder. So I went on digging.

"What kind of time did you do here, Ted?"

"I'm not sure I understand you."

"Anybody who ever did time knows what that means. Ted, except for other ra—for other men convicted of the same sort of thing, did you ever have a friend in this joint?"

Silently he shook his head. Then, as Jim Post put a hand on my wrist to check me, I pointed to the moppers, busily cleaning a floor already immaculate. The chaplain sighed.

I said, "Ted, if you came back here as a class leader things would be just the way they were when you were doing time. The cons still wouldn't give you the time of day."

Jim Post's forbearance seemed to be coming to an end.

"Who do you want, Bill? Machinegun, Kelly?"

"Yes," I said. "An ex-convict, now going straight. A guy who's been in the hole, whose rap sheet is marked incorrigible, who maybe assaulted a guard once. That's the kind of man the other cons will listen to. If he can check his resentments in favor of his freedom, they'll figure they can too. And they are used to looking up to men like that, because those are the men who run the Yard."

"He's right, Jim." Ted was standing up, speaking softly. Holding out his hand, he said, "If there's anything else I can do, let me know. I really want to help."

I shook the limp hand, then Jim called a guard to take Ted out of the joint. The mop-pushers drifted out, anxious to pass the word into the network. Jim said, "You were hard on him, but I guess I see your point. I'll look for the kind of man you want."

We grinned at each other. Then he walked up to the office with me. There were quite a few men waiting to talk to me, among them cons with names like Tall Man Johnson, and Three-D McGee. Real men, with real working nicknames, which were not the inventions of a comic-strip or television serial writer.

Buck Rogers greeted me with a worried look. He spoke to me in a tone of grave concern.

"Hardrock has been saying he wants an interview, if you've got guts enough to give it to him. He's been saying all over the Yard you'll be going out of here in a box. I think he means it."

"Tomorrow," I answered. "Tell him he's the first man I want to see tomorrow."

Chapter 6

'm not a man who panics easily, but I'm not stupid enough to
believe I'm indestructible, either. That night, as I told Pony, I
had to face the fact that my chat with Hardrock the next day
could end exactly the way he promised—with me leaving the
joint in a box. It could end in a lot of other ways too. If I backed
down or leaned for protection on the guard, who was never
far away, it would mean the end of the program. If I invited
a convict friend or two to be present in case I needed help,
I'd be safe and wouldn't be a stool pigeon. But then Hardrock
would have won without even a fight—I'd have labeled myself
chicken. Some of the cons might go on coming to me for help
in getting out and getting jobs, but no one would respect me. I
had to face him down alone.

Pony, because of her long association with the Chessman
case, understood the convict code well enough to follow my
reasoning, and she agreed that I was right. Just talking it over
with her made me feel better.

The next morning, as I kissed her goodbye and left for the joint, I suddenly realized I hadn't made her feel any too good. Pony is a strong woman and she's not given to outbursts of sentiment, but her eyes had tears in them as she waved goodbye to me from in the doorway. Maybe she was wondering whether she'd ever see me alive again. I was sorry I'd burdened her with my worries, but it was done now, and there was no undoing it.

Out at Lansing I stopped into Warden Crouse's office before going into the joint. He greeted me with that careful smile of his and asked what he could do for me.

"Nothing special. I'm just checking in with you."

The smile widened a tenth of an inch. "Don't try to con an old hand, Bill. Something's on your mind."

I just sat down. "Okay. You're right. I've come to ask a favor."

"That's new?"

"This one is. For today, I want you to suspend the rule that all visitors have to have a guard with them at all times."

I think it was Warden Lawes, one of the giants of penology, who first wrote down the rule that prison officers must never say yes or no too quickly. I've noticed that the good ones never do.

When Warden Crouse was ready, he answered me. "Suspend it for everyone, or just for you?" he asked.

"You're kidding me, warden. Just for me, and just during the interviews with the men. When I get to the chaplain's office where the men meet with me, couldn't my guard go to another part of the building?"

Mr. Crouse folded his fingers into a steeple and stared at them. "I gave orders you were to be alone. Alone with the interviewees."

"Yes, but the guard stands right outside the door. The men aren't sure whether he can hear or not. *I* don't think he can, but I don't have to tell you how cautious a man gets when he is doing time."

"No," he said drily, "you don't. Trusting himself half the time is high for the average inmate."

He turned in his chair, stared out the window. "Awful weather, isn't it? Every winter around here seems worse than the one before . . . I'm not stalling you, Bill. I'll make up my mind in a minute. You're doing good work with the men, let me think a minute."

"Of course, warden."

"Bill," he continued after a minute or so, "when you were a con, twenty-odd years ago, and I was a young officer, prison populations were different from what they are now. I don't mean just here at Lansing. Every warden and penologist I meet reports the same thing all over. In your time you were a solid con."

I nodded. He meant it as a compliment.

He went on. "A con was a con and a guard was a guard, and they lived in two entirely different worlds. And the guard's work—not to mention the warden's—was easier. An officer knows where he is with a solid con. But nowadays the inmates are largely punks and stool pigeons, and the prison population surges back and forward, thinking one way today and another tomorrow. It's dangerous out there, Bill, and not in the old way."

"Are you trying to say that I have to have a guard with me all the time for my own protection?"

Warden Crouse gave me a searching look. Finally he sighed and said, "I'm giving orders for the guard to put you in the chaplain's office and go away till you send for him. This one time only, okay?"

I had stood up, smiling my thanks. "Yes, warden."

When I arrived at the office for my interviews, I found Hardrock and another prisoner called Highball waiting in the outside room, where Buck Rogers kept the records for Seventh Step and the chaplain.

The corridor was more crowded than usual, a long line of cons stretching down its length. The guard who had escorted me thus far left me at the door to the outer room and walked away down the corridor. No one spoke, but everyone looked startled. This was an unexpected twist. As I motioned Hardrock and Highball into the inside room, Buck looked at me asking silently if he could come in with me. I shook my head and Buck nodded. He understood that I meant to ride this beef alone. But the last glimpse I had of his face showed me a worried man.

There was a glass ashtray on the desk. I opened the second drawer and put the heavy chunk of glass where I could get it in a hurry.

Hardrock I'd expected. Highball I'd heard of but not seen before. I think he'd gotten the nickname because he had once been a brakeman on a railroad. The word was that he was a punk. I was surprised at how big and muscular he was. Most punks are forced into a homosexual role by stronger cons. Highball apparently had taken it on out of choice, for money or advantages. The fact that Hardrock was his jocker was impressive. If Highball, who was strong enough to choose his jocker, thought Hardrock was a useful ally, Hardrock might well be stronger and tougher than I'd realized.

Highball slammed the door shut behind them. He had his sleeves rolled up to show his muscles, and he was wearing a black glove on his right hand, a thick one, heavily ridged with leather seams that would cut deep into any skin they hit.

For a few seconds no one spoke. Then I realized I'd accomplished something I hadn't bargained for. As long as there was a guard in the outer room while they talked to me, Hardrock and Highball had an easy excuse for not killing me. They could always claim they didn't want a new conviction and a year or so in the hole, which is what they would surely get if there were a guard on duty right outside the door to swear I was alone with them when I passed on to my reward. But with no guard on hand and dozens of other cons available as alternative suspects, they couldn't claim that now. I faced them with a steadiness I was far from feeling, and finally they moved. But not toward me.

Hardrock grabbed one of the two straight chairs in the office, pulled it back away from the desk, and sat down. Highball started to move the other chair over toward his jocker, and then thought better of it and sat down at the other end of the desk, in line with Hardrock. He stared at me fiercely and started stroking the glove with the fingers of his right hand. I felt a little better. A tough man hits before he threatens, a mean man tries to bluff. At least one of these guys was only mean. About the other I wasn't sure yet.

Hardrock opened the ball. "You're late," he said.

"I had the see the warden." I didn't say what about. They'd already noticed the guard's unexpected departure.

"Yeah? I though you wasn't going to show at all."

I'd rather lead than be led. "I'm glad you're here. I wanted to see you," I said. "You've been showing up at the Monday night prerelease classes."

"They're open to any con who is eligible."

"They're classes, not shucks. I doubt if you have any idea what they're all about."

"Hardrock, he's saying you're dumb," Highball put in.

I paid no attention to him. "Hardrock, those classes are for guys who want to stay out when they get out. I'm not going to let you foul them up."

"Who's going to stop me?" he demanded. He slid forward on the chair. The way they were sitting, I couldn't keep my eyes straight on him, where they belonged, and watch Highball at the same time. I got my hand near the stashed ashtray.

"I am. It's one thing to push around Jim Emerson, but I'm something else again."

The straight chair creaked as Hardrock shifted his weight. His hand went inside his uniform jacket, and his fingers moved as though he were scratching his belly.

If he was carrying a shiv it would be there.

I pushed my—Chaplain Post's—chair as far back as I could without taking my hand off that comforting ashtray. That way I could watch both of them at one time. Highball was watching Hardrock, waiting for a signal.

Hardrock didn't look at me, and his voice slid into a high whine. "Why pick on me? I haven't done nothing to you."

This was a danger signal. The whine was not weakness. It was meant to get me off my guard. Maybe it was also meant to give Highball time to work up his punk's courage.

I couldn't afford to give him that time.

"You've booked a loser," I said. "You and your punk with his hotshot glove."

I saw the hand under his shirt stiffen.

"Bring your hand out, big shot," I said. "I know what you're thinking. You're thinking Sands has been on the outside, with the bourbon and the broads and the good, rich food so long that maybe he's gone soft. Maybe I have. But cowards don't bet on maybes, only on sure things."

Then I pushed him a little harder. "Supposing you do have a shiv against your paunch. What then? How do you get through the hall out there? The guys will let me handle this beef, because it's mine. But when it's over, it gets to be the beef of every guy who had a hope that I could help him stay out of joints like this, of every guy who hoped I would get him a job on the outside."

Hardrock began sagging. Highball was looking at the floor.

"Make the hall, and then what? You going to spend the rest of your stretch in protective custody? Step on the Yard, and somebody will get you. In the back. For good. Buddy, you can't win."

I let it go there.

Silence came into the office, and grew large. Hardrock finally broke it. "Let's get out of here. The deck is stacked."

They tried to saunter out. But they weren't more than half-way down the hall before I heard laughter. One more big shot had had his sheet torn off, and only a bully had been under the sheet.

Me? I closed the door, sat down, and heaved a sigh of relief. One more crisis in the growth of the Seventh Step program was past history. I even felt a little sorry for Hardrock. But not very sorry.

Chapter 7

Bill? This is Jim Post."

"What can I do for you, Jim?" I asked. From the excitement in his voice even through the telephone, I knew he had something big on his mind.

"Machinegun Kelly didn't answer his phone, but I think I've found someone to help you."

His enthusiasm was contagious.

"Wonderful," I said. "When do I meet him?"

"I'll pick you up after supper and we'll go see him."

The house we drove to later that evening was in another of the numerous Kansas City suburbs—a pleasant-looking place, very well kept up. And the man who opened the door had a pleasant face. He was of medium height and stocky build, his hair, what there was of it, was close-cropped, and his rolled-up sleeves showed tattooed arms. He looked to be a very healthy forty.

He had a good handshake. This may mean nothing, but at least it makes me want to like a new acquaintance.

He said simply, "I'm Joe Wallace. I've heard about you."

Then he stepped back to admit us. No chatterbox this guy. In the living room he waved us to chairs. Then he sat quietly and waited.

Jim Post began.

"I've told Joe about the program, Bill. He hasn't said how sold he is, but he wants to hear more. Right, Joe?"

Joe Wallace solemnly moved a stubborn-looking jaw up and down.

"Well," I said, "shall I start off?"

Very solemnly he said, "It's your nickel."

So I started talking. I'm a salesman, as I've said before, and a good salesman keeps his eyes on those of the prospect, explaining things the buyer shows interest in, cutting short stuff that bores him.

Joe Wallace's eyes were clear, blue, and solemn and they told me exactly nothing.

When I finished, a little lamely, he sat there like a blue-eyed Buddha for what seemed like several long minutes.

Then he wagged the jaw up and down once. "I think it'll work," he said. "I never buy anything until I've had time to think about it. But for some reason I buy you, Sands."

"Bill."

All of a sudden he smiled. His face changed completely. "Okay, Bill." The smile went away. "But now it's my nickel. Maybe I won't fit into your program."

Joe Wallace had been a Main Yard solid con. He'd done five-to-ten out at the Lansing joint and got out on parole. He'd never assaulted a guard or led a riot. But any of the guys who'd been there when he got out seven years before would remember him for two things. He'd operated as a bootlegger all through his time without being caught, and he had got the entire baseball team drunk just before a game.

Jim Post and I laughed till the tears came over Joe's solemn and detailed description of the resulting game, which Lansing lost 14-0, after rolling up what must have been a world's record for errors—dropped flies, missed grounders, balls thrown wide of the wrong base.

"They swung at everything," the deadpan historian said. "Usually before the pitcher threw."

Just as gravely, Joe brought us up to date on his life. He was happily married and had a supervisory position with General Motors in Kansas City, working in materials control. He'd finished parole and was a free man—or, rather, a free ex-convict. "I'll volunteer my time and give Seventh Step a try," he said. "But I've already taken a fall in rehabilitation. A few years ago one of the civic groups here got up a program, but it went flat on its nose."

This conservatism couldn't be answered with a bluster and sales talk. I said, "It's all right with me, but the last word is the class's. If you'll be out there next Monday, we'll let them size you up."

"I'll be there, if the warden will let me in."

Chaplain Jim Post said he would arrange that.

I was already at the prison when Jim brought Joe Wallace into the classroom, so I didn't go through the four locks with him. I'm sure that it was harder on him than it always was on me, just as going into San Quentin would be harder on me.

A lot of the old-timers remembered Joe. Their greeting was warm, and the newer arrivals took their clue from the long-termers. He opened his talk with a wisecrack. "Seven years ago I dressed out of here with ten dollars and a prison-made suit. No money, no debts. A failure. Today I have a closet full of clothes, a good job, a wife, and a house, and I'm twenty thousand dollars in debt. I guess I'm a success."

As Joe talked on, it became apparent that he knew how to reach convicts. He told the story of the caper for which he fell, a completely unsuccessful theft of an empty safe by him and another guy. Unable to lift the safe, they had hired a couple of drunks from a nearby saloon. By the time Joe and his partner got the safe home and cracked it, the drunks had turned Joe in. Joe took the fall, but his partner was never arrested.

He told them too about his first marriage, which had been very unhappy because of his wife's shrewishness. He had submitted to her demands patiently for a long time, but matters came to a head one night at two o'clock in the morning when Joe's wife woke him from a sound sleep.

"I want you to go out and get me a hamburger," she demanded.

"Aw, come on," Joe protested. "It's two o'clock."

Her voice became shrill. "I don't care what time it is! I want a hamburger."

So Joe got up, got dressed, and dutifully started downtown. (They were living in Oklahoma City.) The closer he got to the hamburger stand the angrier he got. So he drove right past it. He drove so far past it that he wound up in Houston, Texas, where he immediately got rip-roaring drunk. He managed to stay drunk for two weeks. Then, when his money was about gone and so were his resentments, he started for home. He arrived back in Oklahoma City at about three A.M. one morning. He called his wife on the telephone and woke her from a sound sleep. When she answered, he said, "Honey, do you want onions on that hamburger?"

That, as it happened, was the end of that marriage.

By eight o'clock, when the class ended, it was obvious that Joe Wallace was in. I was no longer the unique, indispensable man. My principal emotion was relief, but I had a little pang of jealousy too. I'm human.

Joe and I were among the first out of the classroom, and as we started down the hall one of the cons caught up with me and grabbed my arm. I stopped and so did Joe. The con's name was Bo Brown. Bo came to the classes regularly, but he never said much. I didn't know a lot about him.

Still holding my arm, he looked around to see if anyone was in earshot. Joe Wallace promptly got into the doorway, so that we wouldn't be interrupted. Joe was looking better and better.

Bo said quickly, "Sadie's out to get you."

He was talking about one of the head guards, whom the men had nicknamed Sadie—not because he was effeminate, which he wasn't, but as an abbreviation for sadist, which he was.

No time for polite chitchat.

"How do you know?"

"I know his clerk. Sadie got up some kind of paper and got all the lieutenants to sign it. It's gone up to the warden."

"Thanks."

We moved apart, and Joe Wallace quietly let the cons still in the classroom move out toward their cell count.

There was still a light in Warden Crouse's office, though it was long after his normal quitting time, and there were no signs of disturbance in the joint. I knew he'd expected me. He understood the prison grapevine as well as I did. No use aging trouble—it isn't bourbon. I headed in.

As I'd figured, the warden wasn't surprised to see me. All he said was, "Come in for a moment, Bill. I've got something for you. This is a formal petition signed by a number of my guards. Instead of discussing it with me now, take it home and read it. I'll want to see you first thing in the morning, before you start your interviews."

I nodded and put the thing in my pocket. He obviously didn't want to talk any more, so I said good night and walked out to the car where Joe Wallace was waiting.

"If it's any of my business," Joe said, "what's all that about?"

"From now on, everything in the Seventh Step is your business till you say you're pulling out. Remember Sadie?"

Joe nodded, and called him by his right name. "In fifty-three they tried to take Jimmy Thompson to the hole. He put up a fight, and four of the screws finally wrestled him to the floor. When he was down and being held, not before, Sadie beat him unconscious with a lead-tipped club, and kept on beating him after he was out. Jimmy died in the hospital thirty days later . . . Is Sadie what this beef is about?"

"The paper in my pocket is a petition drawn up by Sadie and signed by his yes-men."

I dropped Joe at his house and took the paper home to read.

It was about what I'd expected. Most of it was vague and cloudy, but when you read through the mud, the basic charge was that Bill Sands in particular and the Seventh Step class in general had destroyed the "rapport between the convict population and the custodial staff." Meaning that stool pigeoning had become less popular in Lansing. It ended with the demand that the warden prohibit me from entering the prison any more.

When Pony read it, she blew her top. Bastard was about the nicest thing she could think of to call Sadie. We examined the complaint from every point of view. And finally we found what I could use to turn it against Sadie.

Jim Post was with me when we arrived at the prison the next morning. He too had read the petition and was furious about it.

"What do you think of it?" he asked.

"It's so childishly put together I could eat a small onion and blow it apart."

"I hope you're right," he answered, "because if I know Crouse he'll want it settled promptly."

"That suits me."

When we arrived in the warden's office, his face was somber.

"Bill," he said, "I hope you've had time to think about the complaints that have been made against you in this petition because I'm going to hold a hearing on it this morning."

"That's kind of fast, isn't it, warden?"

"Well, I can't let you back inside the walls until it's settled. That means your work stops until these charges are answered."

"All right, warden, but I have one favor to ask. In view of the fact that the guards had a lot of time to draw this up and I've only had one night to think it over, I would like to present my side of the case at this hearing first."

"That seems fair enough," the warden said. "Let's go."

The warden preceded us to the parole board hearing room, and when we entered, Sadie was already there, surrounded by his cohorts. They were all in uniform and seated on one side of a long mahogany table. There were two chairs directly opposite them, and the warden motioned Jim and me into them.

Warden Crouse sat in the presiding chair at one end of the table. The deputy warden was at the other end, facing him. It seemed to me that the deputy had used a ruler to measure the distance from one side of the table to the other before planting his chair. He was exactly in the middle, impartial until he had heard the evidence.

The dance began. The warden, addressing me very formally as "Mr. Sands," asked if I had read the charges against me. I said I had.

Outside there would be cons mopping the floor, as close to the keyhole as they could get. At least one convict ear would be pressed to the ventilator. The grapevine would be turned on full power.

"All right," said the warden. "Since everyone here has read the charges against you, I think I would like to hear what you have to say first."

It seemed that the deputy rolled his chair a fraction of an inch toward me.

I started off easy—but I was in full voice for the benefit of any unseen listeners. "Am I right in thinking that the leader of your group is—?" I had to use Sadie's right name and title. I hated to. "Or is he just backing up his officers?"

They all looked at Sadie. It was answer enough. He merely grunted.

I said, "Then, unless any of the rest of you object, I'll address my remarks directly to him . . . You spend a good deal of time in this complaint talking about my opening address here, when the whole prison population met in the auditorium to hear me talk about the concepts that were to become the Seventh Step program. Right?"

Another grunt.

I looked squarely at Sadie. "I made a point of looking for you in that audience, but I didn't see you. The truth is, I didn't expect to see you because I had heard that you said you weren't going to go and listen to some ex-convict brag." I gave that a good, meaty wait. Then I asked, "Am I quoting you correctly?"

He could do something more than grunt. His voice was harsh and angry as he said, "Yeah, I said that." He spat his cigarette into a wastebasket.

"Then the part of the complaint based on that speech is pure hearsay and ought to be thrown out. You're complaining about something you never heard except through rumors."

The deputy moved a little more toward Jim Post and me.

"Now," I said, "I'll take up the whole complaint at one time. The charge is that I made and make statements that discourage men from being stool pigeons. And that I air, freely enough, my opinions of what you call correction officers and what I call hacks and screws. Furthermore I accuse them—I repeat it right now—of enjoying keeping men caged, and making them do their time the hard way."

Sadie looked as happy as he could without seeing blood on the floor—convict blood. Obviously he thought that last statement had hanged me. I stared at the table as if I were waiting for him to say something, but he kept silent. I'd done his work for him.

"Okay," I went on. "About stool pigeons. I don't like them. I know a lot of other people who don't either. Do all of you agree that Warden Clinton T. Duffy is a pretty good example of an enlightened penologist?"

Warden Crouse said, "Of course." Sadie gave his grunt. Some of the lieutenants even nodded their heads, very slightly, though not until after their chief had grunted.

"Here's what Duffy said: 'In a girls' boarding school they are called tattletales. In industry they are called backstabbers. In the army they are called traitors. And in prison they are called stool pigeons.' "

"Yeah, but—" began Sadie.

I waited, but that was all he had to say.

"Let me cite another example—General Douglas Mac-Arthur. He was asked to squeal on another West Point cadet, and he put his whole life practically—he was a general's son and an army career was the only thing in the world he ever really wanted—on the block sooner than be a stool pigeon."

The room was very quiet. "Now, I want to ask you a question. You run your prison, unlike Duffy, on the stool pigeon system. And this is certainly your prerogative. But do you really like stool pigeons? When they leave the prison, do you invite them to come as house guests to your home? Do you spend your off-duty hours chatting with them? Or do you avoid them as much as possible, because, like me, you regard them as the scum of the earth? I think you ought to answer that, answer it honestly, because if that's the kind of man you really admire, I'd like the warden to hear you say so."

The deputy moved all the way to our side of the table.

The silence grew and grew. And then it became apparent to everyone in the room that Sadie wasn't going to answer my question. The best he could have said was that he didn't like stool pigeons, but that he didn't know any better way of running a Yard. And with the word of Warden Duffy against him . . .

Still my ball. "Now, we take up what I said about certain types of guards. Certain types, remember. I'm not quoting from memory now, but from a newspaper report of that speech. Incidentally both the warden and the chaplain were there when I gave it. I said that night, 'There are certainly those in the state prison who enjoy brutality, who enjoy inflicting punishment purely for the sadistic thrill it gives them. I don't know who they are, only they and the inmates do. I invite that kind of guard to put on the shoe and see if it fits. If it does, wear it.' "

Still no response. "Here's the clipping if you want to read it. It quotes me as saying that the basic reason for men of that kind working in a prison is the low pay scale. Do you think that the state gives you enough money to hire good men? Do you think that the pay is high enough? Or that the men hired here are the men who would be hired if you could pay more?"

That got a reaction. Sadie spat toward a cuspidor.

Not a single expression of any kind had crossed Warden Crouse's face.

I finished up. "So, I wasn't talking about all guards and custodial officers. Just about the ones who are so beat up by the economic system that they have to take underpaid, unpleasant jobs without futures, and then make up for their own defeat by being brutal, vengeful, sadistic screws. You'd know if you have any men like that on your force. I wouldn't. And once again, I want to ask you—if you do have any, are they the sort of man you admire and invite home to meet your family?"

That should have made him explode, which was what I wanted. If he burst loose he would give himself away and also his attitude toward his job and his prisoners.

But, to my surprise, it was big Jim Post who blew up first, I think he started to say the unchaplainlike word "damn," but it came out "darn." "Darn it, all of you who signed that paper are like a bunch of dogs that someone threw a handful of rocks into. The only ones who yelp are the ones who got hurt . . ."

The deputy said the only thing he said all through the hearing. "Quite so."

Sadie glared at the deputy warden, he glared at the chaplain. Then, finally, he lost his temper.

Sadie's lips worked. Finally he got it out. "All I gotta say is, Bill Sands isn't coming into this prison any more. He's not going to come in!" he repeated, shouting.

The warden pushed back his chair and got to his feet. His voice soft, his face hard, he said, "Perhaps you have forgotten, sir, that I'm the warden of this prison, not you. I am the one who determines who visits here. Mr. Sands can come and go whenever he is on the business of his prerelease class. Is that clear?"

Sadie slowly stood up too. He clenched his hands into fists and rested all his bulky weight on them on the conference table. He started to glare at the warden and then, no doubt, remembered his pension and his job. So he turned and silently lumbered out of the room. The other officers rose and followed him.

When the door closed, Warden Crouse picked up the charge sheets and threw them into a wastebasket. When he turned to me, he wasn't smiling.

"Watch yourself, Bill," he said. I was glad not to be "Mr. Sands" any more. "This time you were right. But let your foot slip, just once, and the program ends. Right then."

I said "Yes, sir" as snappily as I knew how.

The warden and his deputy went out. Jim Post and I waited and then followed them.

Warden Crouse was right. Sadie was not going to give up. He had the time and the staff to rig a tight, tight frame if he saw the chance. From now on I'd walk the high wire at Lansing.

But as we went down the hall, a convict polishing switch plates winked at me, and the hand holding the rag flipped a thumb up in the victory sign.

Chapter 8

The man in the business community who supported the Seventh Step program most strongly was my close friend and creditor, Rue Holland. Rue was a good person to have as a strong supporter, too, because he is one of a family of twelve children (not counting the adopted one), and what one supports they all support. I couldn't have asked for better help. The Hollands have a family unity that far surpasses anything I've ever seen. Perhaps because they get so much love from one another, they have a great deal of love to give to their community. Steve is active in the Little League Football League; Rue was president of the junior chamber of commerce; Keith coaches a kids' baseball team; one brother is a priest, another a marine; one sister is a nun; and they all, in one way or another, give of themselves to other people.

Rue had been attending classes for months, and the Holland construction company had employed as many ex-convicts as they could. When I had a new idea how I might solve the problem of overdue men, naturally I went to Rue Holland with it.

"Rue," I began, "as hard as all of us are working to get jobs for these cons, we haven't changed the overdue situation much. But now I think I've got an answer."

"What's that?" asked Rue.

"The businessmen we get to make that trip to Lansing every Monday night are simply not able to hire all that many men themselves. Most employers won't hire a man sight unseen. But I think a con, if he were on the outside, could get his own job with just a little help from us."

"I'll bet you're right."

"How much will you bet?" I asked. "A hundred bucks? Two hundred?"

"Sure I would. Why?"

Then I explained. "The reason the state won't let a paroled man out until he gets a job is because they figure he's bound to end up stealing. Twenty bucks is the dressing-out dough. How much mileage is he going to get from that? But if someone would guarantee bare living expenses for him, the law wouldn't worry. These aren't hard times. There are plenty of jobs to go around. Two hundred dollars would get him a decent suit, a cheap room and food for a week, maybe two weeks, and enough transportation to get the guy around. Before it was gone, he'd have a job."

Rue grinned. "I see what you've got in mind. Somebody has to put up the dough for the prisoner." He thought a minute, "And the man who had put up the money would take a special interest in him. He'd be his sponsor, say. He'd have a stake in helping his con with advice, and he could pass along job tips too. There'd be a kind of friendly competition to get your man placed before the other guy's. I'll be the first one, Bill, and I'm sure my brothers will go for it. And a dozen other men I know. How do we start?"

I suggested that maybe we could talk the parole board into giving the sponsor program a try if I met with them face to face. After all, there was a precedent for what we had in mind in the Big Brother movement. If it makes sense to supply friends for friendless kids, then wouldn't it make sense to do the same thing for friendless adults?

"Well, it sure does to me," Rue said. "Why don't you take Jim Post with you when you present it to the board? They've known him for a long time, and he's well thought of."

I liked the idea, and so did Jim Post. He set up the meeting, and we drove to Topeka three days later.

The chairman of the board was named Chesley Looney. He had his whole four-man board with him when we were ushered in. They greeted me courteously and listened attentively to our ideas. The meeting was a short one. At the end they assured us that Mr. Looney would issue a memorandum approving the idea the next day to every Kansas parole officer.

When we told Rue Holland the news, he responded with his usual enthusiasm. He promised to see to it that next Monday's class would be attended by a number of sponsors—all of whom would be ready to put their money down on the Parole Sweepstakes. Not that we called it that. It was to have a much more dignified title—The Man-to-Man Sponsorship Program.

I should have been happy, but I wasn't. I had begun to relax after Joe Wallace joined the program and promised to take some of the heavy burden off my shoulders. Until then I had no idea how tired I really was, but as soon as I stopped long enough to take a deep breath, I realized I had been living on nervous energy for months. The strain of holding off creditors from day to day and living under a heavy cloud of debts was coupled with the strain of fighting what I now realized was and had been all along a desperate battle for the Seventh Step program. I'm not saying that the battle wasn't fun—I loved it. But it was often hard and so often discouraging! And it took all I had, sometimes, to keep at it. By now it began to overwhelm me. I developed a tremor in one hand, and friends started telling me I looked sick. I believed them. I felt sick. But at least, I thought, Joe would be taking on a lot of the work that was suddenly too much for me.

And that was when the Lansing authorities announced that Joe would not be admitted to the prison again. That announcement was quite a shock. It wasn't long before I learned the reason for it. It made sense, but that didn't make it easier to take. It seemed that Joe's record had somehow been mixed up in the records room with that of another man of the same name. After getting out, this other man had committed a number of crimes. Some of the charges against him had been filed in our Joe Wallace's jacket. It took five weeks for the Lansing records office to get all of the misdemeanors and felonies of the other Joe Wallace back into the right jacket. Which meant that for five weeks Joe was not admitted into Lansing.

In the meantime, Les Thompson, acting this time as my doctor rather than my benefactor, kept urging me to take a vacation. When I insisted that I was an old hand at bouncing back from exhaustion, he would point out that I couldn't start bouncing back while keeping up a sixteen-, eighteen-, twenty-hour work day, seven days a week.

Some good things happened around this time. I scrounged enough time to go around and talk to each of my creditors in person, and tell them about the program. And without exception they were more interested in knowing that something was going to be done for the poor devils waiting for parole than they were in getting their money.

I remember particularly our grocer, whose name was Carl Arbeiter. His last name means worker, and he certainly was one. He and his wife ran an independent store, and in order to beat out a living in the face of chainstore competition, they threw away the clock and just worked until the last customer was served. The store was, for once, empty of customers when I called on him. I told him what I was doing and asked for a little more time before I started repaying the four hundred dollars I owed him. I assured him that I would pay interest and I offered not to ask him to charge anything more.

He didn't laugh aloud, but his eyes twinkled. "Interest is for bankers, Mr. Sands, and groceries are for grocers," he said. "But I don't like what you said about not adding to your charge account. You mean, just because I have let you charge so far, you are going to take your business elsewhere. Is that fair?"

At my astounded expression, he laughed aloud. Then a customer came in, and he grabbed my hand, squeezed it, and went forward to work his head off making a few cents' profit. And this, mind you, was not in some small town, but in big Kansas City. I'm a Californian, of course, but it seems to me that Midwesterners are the kindliest people in the country.

The Monday of the first session of the Man-to-Man program came at last. Rue had lined up more than a dozen sponsors, each of good character and substantial financial standing.

I told the class, "All of you men with past-due dates have said here in the class that you want to make your freedom permanent. So a bunch of squarejohns have offered to bet their money on you. They're going to take you out one at a time—one sponsor, one parolee. Which puts it right up to you men.

Your sponsor can't walk another man through the front gate till you have paid back whatever the sponsor advanced you. Is all that clear?"

It was clear, all right. A solid con has his code, and the core of it is not to foul up another man's time. In this case it was another man's freedom.

Then I asked the overdue men to please stand. I expected an immediate response, but I didn't get it. For a moment everyone sat silent, just staring at me. Then, hesitantly, Lefty Boyd rose, and then Bill Larson, and then, almost simultaneously, a half-dozen other men. Once that many were up, all the overdue men came to their feet in a rush. I sensed that for the first time the cons were beginning to believe that freedom was really coming their way.

I had known how many men were overdue, but there was a difference between knowing and seeing. The standing men— more than eighty out of a class of well over ninety—made the dozen sponsors look inadequate.

I invited the sponsors to pick their men. Most of them had been to class before, and they knew the men by sight. But they had no way of judging character among convicts. As soon as the selecting began, I saw that I had made a mistake.

John Fisher, a dentist who had attended two previous meetings, had clearly made up his mind before hand. He walked right past Lefty and Wash, and several other men I respected equally, and picked Gene Browning—one of the joint's most notorious punks. I immediately understood why. Gene Browning was only twenty-three years old, a first-time loser, gentle-looking and slight and neat. He looked for all the world like a college senior or a young writer.

When I looked around I saw that the sponsors, with practically no exceptions, were all making the same mistakes.

They simply chose by the signs people use on the outside to judge men. How else could they judge? They had never been convicts.

Naturally I was glad to see any man have a chance at freedom. But I wanted to cry when I looked at the faces of the men being passed over. Bill Larson, for instance, a born optimist who happened to be a many-time loser in his forties, had been among the first to stand. He stood there with a big, happy smile until he began to realize that no one was going to choose him. I watched that happy smile fade, as he tried to adopt an attitude of indifference. It didn't quite come off. When the choosing was finished, he walked up to the young nice-looking punk, Gene Browning, and said, "Congratulations, kid, don't let us down."

His reaction was typical of the solid-core cons, none of whom was chosen. Pegleg, for instance, was as dependable a man as the Main Yard ever saw. But he had twenty-seven calendar years in the joint behind him and a wooden leg under him: who'd willingly choose him? He just laughed it off. "You can't win them all, and this is sure helping a lot of men." Booker Graham, a Negro, was more forthright. "I should have known," he said. "None of us colored fellows are going to get the nod. If these squarejohns mean so well, why don't they pick the men who have the most need?"

Booker had said it all.

The next morning I asked Buck Rogers to list all the men who were overdue on parole in the order of their parole date and then give me a separate list of the ten with the oldest dates.

When Buck handed me the list, it had a title I liked. "The Ten Most Wanting Men."

While Buck was at work on the details, I went to Rue Holland and asked if I could talk over the program with him and his brothers. He gathered the clan in the construction company's office. I found Rue very enthusiastic about the class the week before.

"Wasn't that great?" Rue asked. "I've told Steve and Keith about it. They're both sorry they missed the class, but they plan to sponsor one man each in the next week or two."

"That's what I came to talk about," I said. "It wasn't as great as it looked to you." I went on to explain what had gone wrong. When I finished, Rue looked at me worriedly. "What can we do about it?"

"I want to make a hard and fast rule that any man who sponsors an inmate must take the one I choose for him. Naturally, the men chosen last week will keep the sponsors they have. But for the future meetings, I will select the inmates entirely on the basis of who is longest overdue, without regard to creed, color, or crime."

The marvelous Holland clan nodded as one.

"There's only one hitch," I continued. "I'm not sure the sponsors will buy it."

"I'm one who will," Steve said.

"So am I," Keith said. "It's the only fair way to work it."

"That's why I'm here. I hoped you'd feel this way. And I'm hoping you can help me sell it to the others."

"Sure," Steve said. "I'll take the first one, and the rest will just have to follow."

While I was hammering out the new sponsorship program, the Lansing office was sorting out the two Joe Wallace jackets. It took five weeks to do it, but finally Joe's freedom of entry was restored to him. Now that Joe was ready to start taking over classes, I really could think of relaxing, maybe even getting away for a few weeks. Les and Barbara Thompson had a cabin in the Rockies which they weren't using, and they offered it as a rest camp. Pony and I were figuring how we could scrape up the money for a vacation, and began to realize that it wouldn't amount to much. We'd be living rent free and not eating any more than we did at home.

Joe Wallace and I both went to the next class where we were to announce the revised sponsorship program. Ten new businessmen were there. Rue had really worked heroically to produce so many, to add to the dozen who had already chosen before we had worked out the new rule. Rue had lined them up behind Steve on one side of the room. It turned out to be fortunate that Steve had missed the last meeting. I made a brief announcement: "The squarejohns who are sponsoring parole men have agreed to a new plan. Instead of each man picking a guy to back, we are going to assign them their men in order of date. First squarejohn?"

Steve slowly stood up.

I asked Buck who had the oldest date.

Buck Rogers picked up the list he had made and slowly unfolded it. "R. B. Hawkins," he read. "Stand up, Arbie."

The cons were absolutely silent. They knew what was coming. So did I. But Steve Holland and the rest of the sponsors were about to be taken unawares.

Slowly, with hesitation and doubt, a small, wrinkled fifty-year-old Negro got off his chair in the back of the room. He raised a hand, and it was shaking. "That's me," he said softly. "I've been waiting almost three years now."

The men leaned forward in their chairs and looked plainly shocked. I knew what they must be thinking. Arbie looked about as unemployable as a man could look, standing there shriveled and frightened, staring at me in disbelief. It was obvious he'd pretty much given up hope. I bulled ahead. "Steve

Holland, meet R. B. Hawkins. Arbie, tell Steve what you're in for, and how much time you've done."

Arbie swallowed a few times. He had his eyes on the floor. "Been in eight years. Judge said I was guilty of rape."

We were lucky that Steve had missed the first sponsorships, that we had him as our first man that night. I think the others might have balked, but Steve was a Holland, and when they go, they keep on going.

Steve just stepped out into the aisle—we all knew that Arbie was too nervous to walk—and strolled back to the little Negro, his hand out. "Arbie, I'm Steve Holland and I'm your friend."

Arbie's shaking hand was completely hidden inside Steve's big fist.

I sat down and turned the meeting over to Joe Wallace, which was a dirty trick. Joe's eyes were as wet as mine, and so were those of a lot of convicts, even the toughest ones.

The rest of the program went off without a stumble. How could it miss with Steve's great example in front of the other sponsors? None of the other parolees looked as hopeless— as old, as unemployable, with such an unsympathetic crime against him—as Arbie.

Nine days later Arbie was dressed out, and Steve was at the gate to meet him and take him to his home. Arbie told me later he hadn't expected that. He thought that he'd be talked to in Steve's office and given a little money for a bed in a flophouse. He said he didn't know what to do with his hands when he found himself sitting down to dinner with Steve and his family, white linen on the table, candles lighting the room. But none of the Hollands seemed to notice his confusion, and after a while he began to feel he'd always lived like this and with this sort of friends.

Two years later Arbie was still out, but Gene Browning—the clean-cut punk who had been the first man selected that first free-choice night—was back in for repeating his crime of car theft.

Incidentally, the "rape" charge against Arbie was not quite that. He had had a common-law wife, and she was seventeen, which is under the age of consent in Kansas. She'd yelled rape during a family quarrel and then couldn't take it back, because having sexual relations with a girl under eighteen is rape, statutory rape, whether she signs a complaint or not. Once it is uncovered, it is an automatic beef. Arbie also had a background of petty crime, but the authorities had not been able to convict him of any particular beef.

After the meeting in which The Ten Most Wanting Men were assigned, Karl Bowen came up to me. He said, "Fifteen minutes till cell count. Got it free, Bill?"

"Sure. Joe Wallace can talk to anybody with questions. It's his class now."

We went into the chaplain's office.

Karl was no word waster. He said, "I told you once I wasn't buying what you sell and you got me to promise I'd think it over. Well, I've thought I want to tell you I've changed my mind. Now I am buying. Jim Emerson has got me a job in a steel mill. More than that, if I make good, they'll take on more men. I don't know how many, but Jim says it might be as many as twenty, maybe even more." As I thought in the beginning, Karl had been a long, hard sell.

He hadn't told me that he "bought" until he had his job and was ready to go. It made it more believable.

"Then you'll make it, Karl," I said. "No solid-core con ever let down twenty other guys. Certainly you're not going to."

He just looked at me out of his dark eyes. Then he shrugged and turned away . . .

We didn't leave for Colorado right away. Instead with Rue, Keith, and Steve handling the sponsorship program, Joe Wallace handling the classes, and both Chaplain Jim Post and newspaperman Jim Emerson taking on almost everything else, I went flat on my broken nose, like a man who has been walking into a high wind that suddenly stopped.

Dr. C. Leslie Thompson did not say "I told you so" until I was out of bed, several days later. But Pony did, and Barbara, when she was allowed to visit me, looked it.

"You leave for Colorado tomorrow," Les said, when he gave me permission to get up and walk around the house. "You and Pony and Bonnie. I've given Pony a check to cover your expenses . . . Don't argue. I'm the one with the medical license. Anyway I've lent you too much money to have you die now. I've got to protect my investment. That's better. Go on and grin. One word of argument, and I'll ship you to the hospital—in a strait jacket, if I have to. And we've got a head nurse out there who outweighs and outmuscles you. She'd just love to keep you in bed a month or two. She seldom gets to fight in her own class."

"Okay, okay, Les. You win. And thanks."

"Shut up, patient."

The next day I sprawled on the living-room couch and observed the whirlwind Pony and Bonnie made as they packed, unpacked, and then packed again, while they speculated—wildly—what the climate and social level of Grand Lake would be, and what they would be expected to wear. Bonnie was still a child, but she was already a woman about clothes.

When the doorbell rang, Pony looked apprehensive. The trip, the vacation, was too good to be true. Something or somebody was about to prevent it. When we saw that it was Joe Wallace—on a day when he should have been working for General Motors—I began to share her fears. The girls disappeared into the bedroom and left me alone with Joe.

He came right to the point. "Bill, I hate to have to tell you this. But I'm dropping out of the program. I'm not going to Lansing any more."

Play it cagey, Bill Sands. Maybe this guy just has a minor grievance. Maybe you can straighten it out. How could this happen? Who could fluff Joe off? Me? Jim Post? Jim Emerson? Buck Rogers?

But under it all was the conviction that Joe was too solid-core to get fluffed off about nothing.

"What the hell's happened, Joe?"

"My wife," he said. "She's afraid that the other kids on the block, in the school, are going to start asking why our little girl's father hangs around prisons and knows so many convicts."

"Ouch."

Joe Wallace nodded, his eyes solemn. "I have to do it, Bill. When we adopted the kid, we swore to the adoption agency and to each other we would always put her welfare ahead of anything else."

"You couldn't do less," I muttered. But I really wasn't thinking about what I was saying. I was thinking about what I was going to say to Pony and Bonnie. The trip was off. The indispensable man was indispensable again. I could feel what I called my "virus" and Doctor Les called my "breakdown" coming back on me.

But there was nothing I could say to Joe. He left, sadly, and I went to break the news to Pony.

She wouldn't change our plans. She threatened to slip me a sedative and have Les cart me off to the hospital in an ambulance. She pointed out—in fact she shouted it loud and clear—that Jim Post, Jim Emerson, and Buck Rogers were still on the job, that Rue and the other Hollands had promised to keep an eye on the program. I answered that most of the men she named were squarejohns. And with Karl Bowen leaving the prison and Joe Wallace quitting, there would be no convict or ex-con available for a prison of leadership. "It would take a miracle," I told her, "a real, no-fooling miracle to keep this program alive if I go away now." She reminded me that I had always said that someday the program would have to stand on its own feet. Well, let it start now.

In other words, we went.

Chapter 9

The Colorado Rockies were a whole new world, a world of clean air and high peaks, pine and spruce and fir trees, a place of deep valleys where white water bubbles over shining rocks, and of peaks where the brain cannot believe how much and how far the eye can see.

Les and Barbara had talked about their "cabin." Pony and I sat and rocked with laughter at the description, while Bonnie ran around discovering new rooms and other wonders, and skidded back to us to report on them.

There *was* a cabin. Les Thompson's father, who had invented the method of musical instruction named after him, had built it. It was the finest one-room mountain cabin I have ever seen. But we were to stay in the guesthouse, a few yards away. Just a little, old nothing. A two-story beamed living room, three bedrooms, two baths, a huge kitchen, and a three-car garage. Bonnie found a twenty-foot sailboat in one stall of the garage, and wanted me to take it out on the lake right then.

Of course, this was just the guesthouse. The main house was up the hill from us. Six bedrooms, four baths, and so on and so forth. Then down the hill from us was the boathouse. A nineteen-foot motorboat lived there. There is nothing like roughing it in the mountains.

Mist came off the lake as night came down, but the air was dry and comfortably cool. Pony fixed dinner, and I ate and went to bed. And for the next seven days that was all I did—eat and sleep. Bunches of tangled nerves along my spine became apparent to me and then slowly unknotted.

When the first week was over I began to feel human. So naturally I decided to crowd things. I got Pony to tow me behind the motorboat on water skis.

I've always been proud of my physical condition. If a man can be said not to have any physical condition at all, that was the shape I was in when we got to Grand Lake. Ten minutes of water skiing behind the motorboat and I dropped off, completely shot. And when I hit the alpine water of the lake, I almost cramped. Pony had to help me into the boat, and even with help, I slipped and cracked my ribs against a cleat.

That night I had a nightmare—the most realistic one I've ever had in my life. I was back in that isolated cell in San Quentin with three guards standing over me, beating me with their lead-tipped canes. The nightmare ended when one guard swung his cane as if it were a golf club directly at my ribs. The pain woke me up. It was the accident of the previous day that caused the pain, of course. But the nightmare had reawakened all the horror of those days and nights in San Quentin. It seemed hours before dawn came, and they were bleak, haunted hours, filled with recollections of pain and frustrated rage and the total aloneness I felt in solitary there.

I hadn't realized how sick I was. I occasionally suffer insomnia, but I had never spent a night like this one since the nights I spent in San Quentin. There the nightmare was real, though. I had thought our Colorado vacation would be a matter of weeks. It stretched out into a month before I was able to attempt a long walk. I did it alone, so no one would know how often I had to stop and rest.

Each day the rests became less frequent, and finally we took out the powerboat again. Now I could stay on the skis an hour. The comeback was well under way when, just after dinner, the phone rang, and my heart thudded. Les and Barbara were the only people who knew the number. Everybody else had been told to call Dr. Thompson's office, and Les had said he wouldn't put a call through unless the sky had fallen.

The voice on the end was as strange as the name the man gave me. Then he said, "I'm Karl Bowen's boss. I thought he might have told you."

"No," I said. "No. If he did, I've forgotten. I've been sick."

I was almost babbling, and I knew it. I forced myself to shut up while the stranger apologized for disturbing me. He knew I'd been sick, he'd had to get the number from my doctor. I only half-listened. The call could mean only one thing. Karl had gone sour on me, on the program, on the other cons who had been promised jobs if he made good. My original reaction was that of a sick man. How could Karl have done this to me?

Then I began to swing back into orbit. "All right, sir. Whatever it is, I'm sure it can be straightened out." Rue or someone could get him another job. So he slipped once. He was still worth another chance.

"What's he done?" I asked.

"Done?" The steel man sounded puzzled. "Why, it isn't exactly what he's done."

All right, pal, I thought, it's your nickel. But I didn't say it. I was going to need this man's help to buy Karl that second chance.

"He hasn't exactly done anything. It's the way he does it. I put him to work tailing steel—that's pretty rough work. He's the first man in in the morning, last man out at night. He does more work than any man on the crew."

"Then what's your beef?"

That touched him off. "Beef is right! His hands look *just* like raw beef. I tried to get him to take two days off, but he wouldn't. He asked me what I was going to do about it? Tear-gas him?"

I began to laugh. Jim Emerson must have told this steel man to call me, and Les Thompson had figured the call would be good medicine. How right they were!

"I can't make Karl take it easy," I said. "you wasted your call."

"Oh, I know. I know Karl pretty well by now. But I figured it out for myself. I'm promoting him to be lead man. He'll be supervising instead of trying to do a whole squad's job himself. That'll give his hands a little rest."

I gulped. Well, a man who's had a bad virus can be expected to have shaky hands and a quavery voice. "Thanks a lot for calling me."

"Well, I'm grateful to you for getting Karl for me. If he's any example of the kind of man your program has to offer, I'll take on a Lansing man any time I've got an opening. And Jim Emerson said you had been ill, and could use some good news."

We said goodbye, and I hung up the phone and sat down.

All I needed to make me completely happy was to see the faces of the Lansing officers who had said Karl was hopeless. Incorrigible, his jacket said. And the faces of the other cons— maybe as many as twenty, Jim Emerson had guessed—who would dress out right into the steel mill. Karl's steel mill. Hell, the rate he was going, maybe it would be his steel mill in a few years.

I didn't think I could get any happier. But there was more to come. The proofs for my autobiography, *My Shadow Ran Fast,* were forwarded to us while we were still at Grand Lake. Registered mail. Valuable stuff. I signed for it, and then Pony and I scrabbled our fingers all over the package trying to get it open.

Galley proofs. Real, professional galley proofs. Long sheets of paper with three or four pages of type on each one.

We had never really believed there was going to be a book until then, I think. It was just something that Pony and I and our friends and the people who believed in me talked about. Then there was the long, painstaking work of proofreading. We started the job of going over every word for typographical errors and errors of fact—wrong names, dates, that sort of thing.

I read first, and Pony followed me. She was a newspaper-woman, and much better at it than I was. I had a tendency to get lost in the story, even though it was my own story. It had been a piecemeal sort of writing. Part of it I'd done, part Pony had done, part we had done together. Read this way, in neat, hard type on glossy paper, there was a sweep to it. An inevitability.

My story had to end up with the Seventh Step movement. Or something like it under another name. I had never had a chance of avoiding my destiny. You could feel that as the story unwound. Just as Chaplain Jim Post had said that Sunday in his house back in gloomy December Kansas. I could see his Persian rug now, in the long sheets of glossy paper.

Dr. C. Leslie relaxed his rules, and I began getting bulletins from Kansas City and from the class at Lansing.

It was the latter that interested me most. Something had changed out there. Despite the absence of the indispensable Bill Sands, attendance was increasing and the little newsletter about the class showed heartening enthusiasm.

A new name began to appear in class bulletins. Ezra Kingsley. "Ezra Kingsley says this."

"Ezra Kingsley was elected class coordinator." And, finally, "Ezra Kingsley is arranging for new quarters for the class."

How long had the chaplain and I tried to get new quarters? And this didn't say "Ezra Kingsley is *trying* to arrange new quarters." It said he was doing it.

Who was Ezra Kingsley?

A letter from Rue Holland supplied the first hard information. Ezra Kingsley was doing hard time, a long stretch of it. It would be years before he was eligible for either parole or discharge. So he had little or nothing to gain from the program personally, and had never come to the classes when Joe Wallace or I had been there.

But after I had gone, he had showed up one Monday night and sat quietly through a whole meeting. After that he moved in, giving advice, suggesting this, advocating that. And the men had listened to him because he had the reputation of being one of the toughest cons in the prison. Now he was just about taking over the class, Rue said. And Rue—whose judgment I usually trusted—thought it was a fine thing.

I found myself looking forward to each weekly bulletin. Then one by one new men were added to the committee, men I didn't know, until the new men out-numbered the old. I began to worry. Were they hard cons, or were they a different breed altogether?

I knew that in the wrong hands the whole prerelease program could disintegrate completely virtually overnight. And everything I had worked for and got others to work for—the Hollands, Jim Post, Jim Emerson, all the sponsors—would be lost beyond hope of recovery.

So there was a good deal of apprehension mixed up with my feelings of hope. The worry overrode the hope when a bulletin was headlined: EZRA KINGSLEY ESTABLISHES NEW FORMAT FOR PRERELEASE CLASS.

All my philosophy, my "cool," went out the window into the clean Colorado sunshine. It was fine to say that something—power, God, destiny, kismet—supplied a new man when an indispensable one became unavailable. It was fine to say that someday Seventh Step would have to travel on its own legs. But a new format? A lot of time, a lot of experimentation had gone into the routine of that class. Nothing had been done without thought and discussion and—on Jim Post's part, anyway—prayer.

Now, in a few weeks, this Ezra Kingsley had changed the format. I could only hope he hadn't changed the basic purpose too, or that if he had, there'd be something I could salvage when I got back.

We started to pack.

Chapter 10

My first day back in Kansas City saw me in Warden Crouse's office.

I asked Mr. Crouse what he could tell me about Ezra Kingsley.

The warden shrugged. "Where do you want me to start? Chaplain Post says that you once said you'd like to use Machinegun Kelly in your program. Ezra Kingsley comes as close as anybody in this penitentiary. For one thing, he was really bigtime on the outside."

"Every prisoner is, to hear him tell it," I said. As any criminologist will tell you, the average income from crime is a few hundred dollars a year.

Warden Crouse laughed. "I know. But the robbery for which Ezra fell—this time—netted him more than fifteen thousand dollars. He came into this place with a price on his head, for operating bigtime on the outside, and kept right on operating inside. He used to cause me and my staff a lot of trouble."

I sat up a little straighter. "Used to?"

"For a year Ezra Kingsley's record has been absolutely clean. Spotless."

All I knew about joints and Main Yards and convicts and inmates ran through my head. I could think of several reasons why a hard con would suddenly straighten up—or at least pretend to. Not all of them would qualify a man for leadership of the Seventh Step.

The warden went on. "Now, here's something about Ezra Kingsley that will really surprise you. He is totally honest, in the sense that his word can always be counted on. He will not lie under any circumstances."

"A stool pigeon?" It sounded like it, but I couldn't believe that even an innocent like Jim Post would let one of that nauseating breed take over the class. But the warden was laughing. He knew what I thought of stool pigeons, and it is probable that he had the same opinion. Certainly nothing that had happened at the confrontation with Sadie had made me think otherwise.

"Far from a stool pigeon," he said. "Just the opposite. When I ask him if he knows about something going on in the Yard, he won't even say he doesn't. Too honest to do that. He always gives the same answer: 'I know, warden, but I won't tell you.' And he won't. It's got so I've given up asking."

I arrived at Jim Post's office with a lot of impressions of Ezra Kingsley. I found Jim, once we had greeted each other, as anxious as anyone else to talk about Ezra. But Jim had pulled Ezra's jacket for me to read, and I asked him not to tell me anything more until I had read it. I needed some hard facts after all the generalities and rumors.

All right. Ezra had spent part of every year since he was nine locked up. He was thirty-nine now. That meant a lot of time, enough to break most human beings. Certainly it was enough to build up a wall of resentment that would rival Boulder Dam.

When his career started, at age seven, Ezra was jiggering. In case you don't know what this is, Ezra's father was on the take, stealing equipment in the oilfields. Ezra's job was to sit in the car and jigger the horn lightly if anybody approached. But he didn't go to jail till he was nine, and then it was for a solo act. His father wasn't involved because the elder Kingsley was already in jail for grand theft. Ezra was caught stealing a pair of fur-lined gloves from a dime store. He'd always wanted good warm gloves, but his father had never taken enough to afford them.

There wasn't any juvenile lockup in Apache, Oklahoma, in those days. There probably isn't now, since the town is still somewhere between a thousand and twenty-five hundred in population.

So they held Ezra in the tank, jail language for a series of cells, all opening on the same corridor. The cell doors were left open. Mr. Kingsley had a chance to punish his wayward son. He took his belt and beat Ezra unmercifully, not for stealing and not for getting caught—but for bothering with such small loot as a pair of gloves, even if they were fur-lined. By the time he was eleven, Ezra ran away from his unsuccessful father. The boy was determined to be a success. A successful thief, that is.

There is, of course, no such thing. But Ezra couldn't know that yet.

Ezra took plenty of money, but he took plenty of falls, too. First he went to reform schools, then to adult joints. Little Houses and Big Houses, they used to be called. He escaped, was recaptured, drew parole and violated it, was chased by the police, and chased other gangsters.

Ezra Kingsley first honored Kansas City when he was thirty.

By this time he was a thoroughly professional thief. He was taking several thousand dollars a week, mostly by armed robberies of supermarkets. He had the kind of a drug habit that the underworld calls an "oilburner." It took a hundred dollars a day just to satisfy his craving. He bought a nightclub so he would have a comfortable hangout. He bought his own bonding company so he would be sprung quickly when he was caught.

The syndicate that ran crime in Kansas City didn't appreciate Ezra's brand of supercrime. It put too much heat on the local boys. So somebody called Ezra Kingsley and told him to get out of town. Obviously they didn't know Ezra very well. He bought an elephant gun and declared a one-man war on the mob. I'd say the odds were about even.

But there is no fairness in gangland. The syndicate upset the odds by buying enough law to have Ezra and one of his friends imprisoned on illegal convictions. The friend's name was Carl Fry. He appealed the illegal conviction, and after a couple of years he was released on a reversal by an honest judge. Two days after he dressed out, Carl Fry was gunned down by syndicate hoods.

The judge refused to reverse Ezra's sentence, though it was just as illegal as Fry's. Perhaps the court had heard about Ezra's determination to take up syndicate-hunting if he got out. Before he had been framed, he had, among other things, chased the head of the mob down a Kansas highway at better than a hundred miles an hour, holding the wheel with one hand and firing a gun with the other.

So Ezra was doing twenty years at Lansing. The man was a philosopher. He settled down to do his time the good way.

Guards got a hundred and eighty-seven dollars a month in those days. Ezra bought a couple of them to run his errands and wait on him—to be his "horses" in prison language.

Unlike many narcotic addicts, Ezra liked to drink. He says he was seldom sober during his first eight years in Lansing, and usually he drank bonded whiskey. He took over the narcotic smuggling and selling business in the Yard. He also became the principal enforcer there. An enforcer in prison is the man who collects bad debts for other prisoners. Some of the debts are for cigarettes loaned, some are for card debts, some for bets on outside sporting events. It didn't matter to Ezra. For fifty percent he would collect for anyone, from anyone, including former clients and penitentiary bigshots like Hardrock.

Ezra didn't—doesn't—know what fear is. And everyone in the Yard knew it.

Some of this I got from talking to Jim Post and the men in the Yard, some from Ezra Kingsley's jacket. The prison record could just about be summed up in the one word written large on the sheet. INCORRIGIBLE.

But . . .

Ezra had broken his narcotic addiction, what the men called his "oil-burning habit." Just decided to quit—and did it. Enough has been written, screened, and broadcast for every citizen of the United States to know all about drug addiction. If an addict wants to quit, he needs doctors, an infirmary, substitute drugs, and time. And even then it's a painful process. Ezra had none of those things, except time, and he had plenty of that. Ezra didn't try to get any of the other props. He quit cold turkey, as addicts put it. Men on the Yard told me about it. Jim Post had also heard the tale.

Ezra would leave his cell after a night without feeding his habit. The minute he tried to move, his face would drip with sweat. He couldn't walk down the corridor of the cell block except by clinging to the iron, a rung at a time. In this way he would make it to mess hall, eat something, retch it up, drink some coffee, lose that, and call it a meal. When the withdrawal pains hit him he would grab the nearest object and hang on. If he grabbed wood, it was likely to splinter from the terrible pressure of his finger grip, and Ezra has small hands for a man his size.

He made the cure that way, the hard way. And, according to Yard legend, he did it with a fresh fix of heroin and a needle inside his gray uniform at all times. He never used it.

A year ago he decided to get smart and quit fighting the system. I asked the chaplain about that. Jim is full of Christian charity and his answer was typical. "I think Ezra is a sincerely changed man. I believe in him and I think he is the best thing that could have happened to the class."

That was to be seen. I have led a rougher life than the chaplain, and I am a good deal more cynical.

The office where I was to meet Ezra Kingsley for the first time was a half-glass door. I sat so I could look down the hall through the glass.

The minute I saw Ezra Kingsley I knew who he was. An Italian criminologist named Lombroso spent a good deal of time proving that he could tell criminals by their appearance. That theory blew up more than fifty years ago. There is no such thing as a criminal type, a criminal face. Yet Ezra Kingsley looks like a convict. He is not pretty. His thick close-cropped hair is black, except for a white streak near his left temple where a scar from a bullet runs from his forehead under the hairline. There are a couple of knife scars visible on his face, too.

Still, even in prison gray, he carries himself with assurance, with an air of authority and purpose. He is about six feet tall, but so well-muscled that he looks stocky.

Inside the door he grinned at me, and suddenly, he *was* handsome, after all. We exchanged names, unnecessarily, and he pulled a chair around and straddled it, arms crossed on the back. "What can I do for you?" he asked.

That was a setback. I was used to doing things for convicts. This one was offering to do things for me. But there was nothing challenging in the very direct gaze he'd put on me. He was too self-confident to challenge. There was no use in a couple of men like us trying to stare each other down. I suspect that if we had tried it, we would have been there till Ezra was due to go out on flat time.

So I swung back. "You can tell me why you came out of the Main Yard with the kind of rep you've got and took over the Seventh Step, class and committee and all."

"Fair enough," Ezra said easily. "I want to get out of this joint. Your movement brings squarejohns out here to help men get out. If I have to help a lot of other men in order to impress some square bigshot that I ought to be helped myself, fair enough."

"You're using the movement as a shuck," I said.

Ezra's dark gaze didn't flinch. "Okay, if you want to put it that way. But you say a man doesn't have to get moral, he doesn't have to turn religious. All he has to do is want to get out."

"And stay out."

Ezra nodded. "That's me. I am through, Bill. I've spent almost half my life in the joints. By the time I finish this hitch, it'll be more. When I get out I intend to stay out."

There was no doubt that Ezra had helped the class. There was no doubt that he was valuable to the movement. And Warden Crouse had said that the one thing that Ezra would not do was lie. But I had to pin him down. I said, "You're through taking then, Ezra?"

"Through. Finished. Washed up."

I looked at him without saying anything for a minute or two. Then I said: "You have a reputation for being honest, I hear. So I'll take your word for it."

Ezra didn't change his expression.

"So let's talk about the prerelease class. What's the idea of the new format? Wasn't the old one good enough for you?"

Ezra smiled a little. "No, it wasn't, but the changes aren't as drastic as you might think. Just one maybe."

"What's that?" I asked.

"You used to have a man who had a problem to air stand in his place and talk to you about it. Now, anyone who wants to talk comes up to the front and talks to the whole class."

"Is that all?"

"Not quite. We have a new rule. Anyone in the class can interrupt at any time and tear the sheet off the guy who's talking."

"That sounds as if all hell would break loose when some phony is talking."

Patiently Ezra explained, "No, all hell doesn't break loose. I control the interruptions. When a man wants to comment, he has to raise his hand and wait to be recognized. When a real phony is talking, I see more hands than a busy manicurist."

"So far so good. Now, what about the new guys on the committee? I got along with two men. Why do you need five?"

Ezra smiled again. "When you were laid up, you didn't see the bulletin for a while, did you?"

"No," I said. "What's that got to do with it?"

Ezra handed me the back issues I hadn't seen, and asked me to look at the little box in each issue that lists the number of men in attendance.

I saw at once what he was getting at. The week after I had left for Colorado, there were eighty men at class. The following week only sixty-eight showed up. The figure decreased steadily to the low point of twenty-three, and then began to rise. At the most recent class there was a hundred and seven men.

"When you came out here every Monday," Ezra explained, "a lot of guys turned out to see you and hear you. But when you left, it had to be taken over by the convicts, or it would have gone down the drain. That makes it too big a job for two cons. I needed more and I got them."

Was this guy just too good to be true? I sat thinking about it for a minute. Then I said, "All right. You have my full backing, in the committee and in the class—as long as you're right. Go wrong, and I fight you."

Ezra thought this over, his arms still crossed on the back of the chair. Then he unwound, stood up and put out his hand, and we shook. "It's a deal," he said.

As he was leaving, I suddenly called him back.

He stood in the door. "Yeah?"

"Ezra, you're a pretty damn-funny-looking miracle," I said.

His left eyebrow went up. Then he shrugged and went out.

Chapter 11

Next Monday, Ezra met me at the door of the classroom. The minute we crossed the threshold, I was swamped by old friends—Rue, Steve, and Keith Holland were all there, as was Jim Emerson. Most of the convicts were new to the class. Except for the few I had met before in the Main Yard, I didn't know them. I glanced at the board listing The Ten Most Wanting Men, and looked for the oldest date. It was only three weeks past. I felt sheer pleasure at being back at my life's work, coupled with gratitude toward the Holland family and all the others who had been responsible for taking our first class, with all its overdue men, out of this bleak place.

Then I noticed four men in prison whites scattered around the room, and for the first time I observed that Ezra wore whites, too. In most prisons, whites are worn by office workers, kitchen hands, and infirmary assistants when on duty. At other times these men wear the standard gray prison uniforms because they're easier to keep clean. I asked Ezra what the white uniforms represented.

"The committee," he said.

Two were from my first committee—Buck Rogers and Henry Cockerham. The two I didn't know were introduced as Otis Brimmer and Horace Winger. Otis was a burglar and Horace an armed robber.

It was time for the meeting to start. The men were taking chairs, settling down. Ezra took the stand, and opened with what we called the Purpose.

We, in this room, share together the desire to live together constructively in a free society. We hope to be forgiven, and we practice forgiveness ourselves. With that thought in mind, we will now greet the man next to us with the knowledge that he, like ourselves, is sincere in attending this meeting. Now give yourself and your neighbor a big hand.

The purpose of these words goes much deeper than just warming up the meeting, making all the men attending participate at once. It attacks the stiff walls of prison prejudice, breaking down the lines of Main Yard cliques. Of course, there are cliques every place. In a school, in a country club, in a chamber of commerce, in politics. But I submit that nowhere are they so strong and clannish as in prison Yards.

Mostly the population breaks down according to the nature of the offense for which each man is serving. Despite the fact that it is very bad penitentiary manners to ask a man why he fell, everyone finds out soon enough.

Then, behavior inside determines other dividing lines. Solid cons will not associate with stool pigeons or the weakling punks, and within their ranks there are further divisions.

But for the purposes of Seventh Step, a prisoner is a prisoner, inmate or hard con, pick-pocket or murderer. All the movement asks is that a man want to change, to get out and stay out. Preconceived notions—pickpockets are weak, check-writers are not interested in reform, stool pigeons are permanently committed to their loathsome way of life, and the rest of them—have no place in a Seventh Step meeting.

So the man-to-man greeting, the neighborly applause, is like a damp rag wiping clean the slate of prison prejudices.

The routine followed at that meeting is the one that is still followed in Seventh Step classes.

After the Purpose, Ezra asked all the men to stand, and following his lead, they recited the Seven Steps in unison. That was a new wrinkle. It was impressive—and I'm moved to this day whenever I hear them do it—because it is done by a group of tough, usually cynical men, reciting their "lessons" like very sincere children. It gets you, listening to it.

Men who were at the class for the first time were introduced—first the visitors, then the new inmates. They were applauded. This took about three minutes.

Then Ezra said, "For the benefit of the new members, I want to explain the ground rules here. For the past seven days, we five committee people have been getting around among the class members, talking to you men and listening to your beefs. At a committee meeting yesterday we picked out the men who have problems that a lot of you have. Or maybe the kind of problem most of you are interested in hearing about. Only the committee knows who's going to be called, so these are not rehearsed talks. All you guys know this program is supposed to help us think realistically about what our lives and problems will be like outside. If any of you hear a guy lying to himself, or wrapping himself in a sheet, do him a favor. Raise your hand immediately and I'll recognize you. Then rip the sheet off. Understood?"

Without waiting for an answer, he continued, "Bob Washington, come up here and tell the class what you've got on your mind."

A heavyset convict who appeared to be in his mid-forties slowly stood up and walked to the speaker's stand. Ezra stepped off to one side.

"Hell, Ezra," Bob muttered, "I ain't got nothing to say."

Seven hands shot up. Smiling, Ezra pointed to a man who was waving frantically, and he stood up.

"Bull!" he exploded. "I'm your cellmate, and you sure as hell have plenty to say when I'm trying to sleep. You been bending my ear about how those squarejohn bosses on the outside won't ever give you a chance. Tell all the guys what you keep telling me every night."

Washington frowned. He looked to be on the verge of anger.

"Well, I ain't told you nothing that ain't true. All I got to say is that I tried to go straight the last time I got out. So when my boss finds out I'm an ex-con, he fires me. Every time I look for another job, they won't hire me because I'm an ex. You gotta lie to them people out there or you don't work. It's a lousy phony bunch of people."

Another forest of hands. Ezra pointed and a man stood up.

"Bob, I know why you were fired from that job you're talking about, and you know it too. You were drunk three days in a row. And I know that that boss bad-talked you every place you looked for work after that. Hell, you never told them people you were an ex-convict, and you ain't got no sign hanging around your neck that says so. Get straight with yourself. Ain't I telling it the way it is?"

Washington's frown deepened, and he muttered, "Well, yeah."

His tormentor continued.

"Look at them squarejohns over there, Bob. Those guys come here when they could be home with their wives. They're finding jobs for us and they sponsor guys like you and me. Do you think they're phony too?"

That got to Bob. He was embarrassed and it made him furious, so that he turned on Ezra.

"Have you got some damn rule says I gotta stand here and take this kind of crap?"

Ezra gave him a friendly smile and laid a hand on his shoulder.

"Take it easy, Bob," he said. "I know this is your first meeting and it seems kind of hard on you. But there's no one here who doesn't want to help you. That's what this is all about. As a matter of fact, Bob, the reason I called on these guys is because I figured they might just make you lose your temper. That's one of your problems. You just don't hold your mud. When your boss bugged you on the outside, you couldn't blow up at him so you went out and got drunk.

"You've just helped a lot of men in this class without knowing it. A lot of us have the same problem, and when we see it in you, we see it in ourselves. I'm one of those guys, Bob, and you've just helped me. Between now and the next class, several of the committee men will come and talk over this problem with you privately. A couple of weeks from now we're going to ask you to talk again, and see what kind of progress you've made in your thinking."

Ezra turned toward the class and said, "I think Bob deserves a big hand, don't you?"

The class responded with real enthusiasm, and the applause lasted until Bob had got back to his seat.

I thought to myself, that was beautifully handled. Score one for Ezra.

Horace Winger had replaced Ezra at the podium, and the second the applause for Bob Washington ended, he said, "The next man we want to hear from is an old hand at this. This is his ninth meeting, and he goes out in the middle of next week. Wrestler, come on up here."

The committee was running the meeting with clockwork precision, without the slightest suggestion of delay. I've seen professional shows with longer stage waits. By the time Wrestler, a man whose nickname was a perfect description, reached the podium, Horace had stepped aside to make room for him.

Wrestler spoke with assurance.

"Like Horace said, I been coming to these meetings for a lot of weeks. You guys really helped me. When I get on the outside, I'm going to try to practice the Seventh Step. I've already talked to my parole office, and I asked him if he'd let me visit with some of the tough young kids in the county jail. I think they'll listen to me, and maybe I can help some of them straighten out. He's agreed to arrange it for me."

A hand went up.

"I think that's a shuck. I think you're lying to us and lying to yourself. You don't want to give us anything to pick on. What do you say to that?"

"What I say is, I think you're trying to get me angry. You did that four weeks ago, but you aren't going to do it now. I mean what I say, and any of you guys who know me well, know that's true. And you know I'm going to have to find a job. I expect to have some trouble. I think there's some truth in what

Bob said, about outsiders not wanting to hire an ex-convict. Particularly one who looks like me."

He smiled.

One hand went up. Horace pointed and the convict got up. "I'll ask you the same question, Wrestler, that we asked Bob," he said. "What about these squarejohns sitting here—do you think they're prejudiced against you?"

"Of course not," Wrestler answered easily. "One of those squarejohns is my sponsor. But there are only twenty-three of these guys here, and I don't think everybody on the outside feels the way they do. I'll make it out there, though. I carry my little card with the Seven Steps printed on it on me all the time. I read them once in the morning, and it's the last thing I do before I go to sleep at night. It might be corny, but that's the way it is. I'd rather be a cornball on the outside than a hipster in the joint."

Horace stepped to Wrestler's side and addressed the class.

"Those of you who weren't here nine weeks ago, when Wrestler first came, can't know that Wrestler found it hard to talk and that he lost his temper easily. And he didn't have any real idea of where he was going or what this class was about. His big problems were with step one and step five. I think he's changed, and he has his resentments under control. I'm proud of him and I'm glad he's going to be one of the guys to represent us on the outside. I know all of us will be pulling for him, and now let's give him a big hand."

Once again the applause was genuinely warm.

Several speakers followed in quick succession, and I was amazed by the eagerness with which they laid their intimate frustrations and resentments out before their fellow convicts. When six of them had talked and been talked to, I looked at my watch. An hour and a quarter of the two hours allotted to the class by the warden had been used. Ezra stepped back to the podium and said, "Now that we have Bill Sands back with us, we can use another part of what the committee has planned as the permanent meeting format. We haven't been able to use it before now because we haven't had an ex-convict who has made it on the outside in regular attendance. But from now on, we assume that Bill will be with us. And if he leaves us again, he'll leave us with some ex-con we can depend on to be here each Monday night. Bill," he said, looking directly to me, "we on the committee think this is important, because an ex-con making good on the outside can give us the next bit of help we need. What I want you to do is to comment on what you've heard here tonight. If we're off the track, tell us so. Maybe some of the squarejohns who are here will tell us the same things you might say, but we can't identify with them. You've been through it and we'll listen."

He turned back to the class and said, "I'd like to call our founder, Bill Sands."

I got to my feet and walked to the speaker's stand.

"Thank you, Ezra. When I left here this was almost a one-man show. I want to tell you that the class is five hundred percent more effective now than it was then. The changeover that we worked for has happened—it's no longer my class, it's yours. However, I'm glad to notice that some things haven't changed. All the cons still say hello to me, and Sadie and most of the guards are still acting as if I'd go away if they don't notice me."

That got a laugh. I went on.

"I noticed that most of you who talked were concerned about getting a job and telling the man who's doing the hiring that you're an ex. First of all, you must be able to do the job you're applying for as well as, no, better than any of the other men who want that job. Don't kid yourself about your qualifications, and then you'll be sure you won't be trying to kid the employer. Please notice that I said 'trying to kid.' Chances are ten to one that he has been hiring men for that particular kind of job a long time—he'll catch on pretty quickly whether or not you really understand the work and can do it.

"Take your time, answer all of his questions, really sell him on how completely you'll fill his needs. When you've got him completely sold, that's the time to tell him you have served time in the state penitentiary. No matter how rough the job is, don't tell him in joint language. And right after you break the news, tell him how you joined the prerelease class of Seventh Step in order to change yourself into a man who can live in a free society.

"Perhaps he's read about Seventh Step in the papers. We've had good publicity. But no matter what he knows be sure to tell him that so far it seems as if most of the men in the program have made it, and you hope you'll make it too. In fact, tell him you're a hundred percent sure you will. Then you'll have to live up to your promise.

"Don't crawl, don't preach. Be on the level. Take out your Seventh Step card and show it to him. Tell him that you will have the extra advantages of outside counseling, both through Seventh Step and from your parole officer. Give him the name of the parole officer, and put a Mister before it.

"Then tell him that statistics show that a man who comes out of prison is almost always extremely loyal to the first employer who trusts him. Finally, say to him, 'Sir, there are still people in this world who demand that I go straight but will not give me the opportunity to do it. These people want to see me wear my ball and chain or my invisible stripes forever. For them, a pound of flesh is never enough. I know you're not that kind of man, or you wouldn't even be talking to me.'

"And then shut up and turn it over to him. If he is willing to name himself a bigot, you don't want to work for him anyway. But if he's on the square, you'll get the job—if you are really qualified. Which is where we started. Don't try and con yourself into a job you can't fill . . . Do you have any questions about what I've said so far?"

There were none.

"I hope someday to see a class like this one operating in every penitentiary in the country. You guys have promised to maintain your freedom, and I will promise to dedicate the rest of my life toward spreading the movement that we have started here. I agree with Ezra that we need a successful ex-con to put in charge of each prison program. I'll go one step further than that. We need *you,* and I personally am depending on each of you to fill that need."

As I walked back to my seat, I knew how the cons who had spoken earlier had felt. No response I ever received as an entertainer was as sweet as the applause I heard that night from my friends in prison.

Ezra took the podium and read the closing thought that we had always used to end the meeting.

Each of you as an individual has only the strength of one. Each of you, as a member of this group, has the strength of many. I believe sincerely that each of you can honestly use that strength to maintain your freedom. I believe in all of you and I further believe that none of you will let all of you down.

Ezra had timed the class so that it ended a few minutes before the guards came in. This timing has been followed in all Seventh Step classes ever since, because it gives the inmates in the class and the law-abiding sponsors who are in attendance a chance to talk to one another and get acquainted. Suddenly the guards came in and started lining the men up to be returned to their cells. Each time this happens I have the same mixed reaction of sadness and exultation. Until that very moment, the room was full of good men who were honestly trying to find the truth and, in so doing, help each other. Suddenly, my friends were convicts again. It was particularly heartrending to see Ezra and his committee, none of whom was eligible for parole (Ezra had arranged it that way to ensure long-term continuity and unselfish service) being herded back to their cells.

The feeling of exultation is never quite equal to the sadness.

Chapter 12

Wayne Bethea had served nine consecutive years when he was released. Forty-eight hours after he dressed out, his landlady called me and said she was worried. "Mr. Bethea won't come out of his room."

That was not too rare. After nine years of being locked up, a man can find the free world pretty terrifying. Pony and I hurried over there. The address proved to be that of a big old mansion, painfully maintained, in what had become a slum of Kansas City. Wayne is a Negro, and so was the landlady anxiously waiting for us on the splintery front porch. A decent, work-worn woman, she was now obviously very much worried.

She blurted out her story. "Mr. Bethea's spent all day and most of yesterday scrubbing his room. I can hear him in there, and he let me in once—but—but—I was almost afraid of him. This isn't the Muelbach Hotel, but I keep it clean and—why what Mr. Bethea is doing is crazy. He's even scrubbed the paint off part of the wall."

"I don't think anything's very wrong, ma'am," I said. "He's been in a cell for nine years, and he washed that cell down every day. It was his home and his job, all at once. It's a habit, and it will take him awhile to break it."

The woman led us upstairs and showed us the door to Wayne's room. She was right. The hall was clean enough, and there was a faded but spotless carpet on the stairs. She kept a clean house. When I lifted my hand to knock on the door, the landlady scurried back downstairs.

Wayne opened the door cautiously, and then recognized me. "Why, Bill. I'm sure glad to see you." Then he saw Pony, and his mobile face changed. He looked more embarrassed than anything else.

If Pony noticed his embarrassment, she didn't let on. "Aren't you going to ask your friends in to see your home?"

Wayne stood aside—what else could he do?—and we were in. He looked around nervously and said, "It isn't much, but it's clean."

I said, "That's what worried your landlady and made her phone me. She was afraid you'd wash through the wall and fall out on the street."

Wayne laughed a little nervously.

"Think of her reputation for running a clean house if that happened," Pony said.

Wayne motioned us to the only two chairs in the room, straight kitchen ones. He sat on the edge of the bed and the edge of his nerves. He was wound up tight as an English umbrella.

I looked around the room. The chairs, a chest of drawers, a bed, a sink, and an icebox. There wasn't even room for a table—the chest of drawers had an electric hotplate on top of it. It was a light-housekeeping room, just barely. But it was bigger than a cell. And there were no guards watching Wayne, no bars for them to watch him through.

"I think I know what's bugging you," I said. "You think everyone is watching you, like you're a bug under a microscope. Right?"

He nodded glumly. He opened the icebox—the lump of ice in it was nearly melted. He took out a plate of fried eggs and sausage, heavily rimmed with congealed grease.

"I bought this stuff on the way here from the bus station, but I couldn't eat it. Last food I swallowed was out at the joint. My first free-world chow, and I can't swallow it." He looked as though he might cry. "Too nervous," he explained unnecessarily.

"Did you come out on the sponsorship plan, Wayne, or did you have a job before you got out?"

"I had a job," he answered. "I'm suppose to start as a hotel bellboy tomorrow. The captain's sort of a cousin of mine. He got me the job, but if he knew the shape I was in he'd fire me."

And if he got fired, he'd go back to Lansing. His parole officer would have some latitude there. He could give Wayne a little time to look for another job. But how could Wayne look for a job if he wouldn't—or couldn't—leave his morbidly clean room?

"Nobody's riding the broom on you, Wayne. It's all in your own mind, which hardly makes it any easier to stand. But come on out with Pony and me, and we'll show you."

First we took him to the most crowded supermarket we knew. Pony gave Wayne a list of things she wanted, and we dispatched him down the most thickly populated aisle, his knuckles tense on the pushbar of the market basket.

At first he went and stopped, pulled back, tried terribly hard to keep his basket or his body from touching anyone else.

But it was double-stamp day, or markdown day, or one of the days when bargains prevail in supermarkets, and the housewives were too busy looking for rare and wonderful buys to mind a little contact.

Gradually Wayne got bolder, got into the spirit of the thing. He became as much a grocery hound as the other shoppers, sniffing out the items Pony had asked him to get, pushing past people, filling his basket. Of course, Pony had sent him after the most commonly used things, the things that would be on the most crowded counters and incidentally, the things we could afford and had to have.

By the time we joined him at the checkout counter, he was grinning. "I'm the invisible man. Nobody hardly looked at me."

"You've got it made, Wayne."

But he didn't. When we drove him downtown, he wouldn't get out of the car. We could have made him get out by force, the two of us pulling on his arms. But that could have attracted police attention, and being questioned by a cop was hardly what Wayne needed.

So we took him home. I broke a rule I'd made when the parolees and discharges started using our little home for a semiclub. I now gave one of them a drink. Two drinks, in fact.

While he was drinking them, Pony cooked up a huge steak. But he couldn't swallow more than the first bite. He said his throat had clamped up on him.

Which didn't stop him from talking. We encouraged him to say anything that came into his head—the psychoanalysts call it free association. Maybe one of them could have made something out of all he said. We didn't even try. We just asked questions to get him started when he stopped.

He told stories about his childhood, stories about men, he'd known inside, stories about jobs he'd had outside. Just anything that came into his head. And, gradually, he began to feel better again. At two o'clock he told Pony that he'd appreciate it if she's heat the steak up for him.

That was his first food in forty-eight hours. He gulped it down, chewing and grinning at the same time. When it was all gone, he put his head back and laughed and laughed, but not hysterically.

At seven in the morning he stood up, thanked us, and asked if we would drive him to the bus stop. "It's time for this working stiff to get at it," he said.

When the bus pulled away, he was staring at us from the rear window. Now he looked not at all like the cheerful man who had eaten in our house. He was once again scared and lonely. But he was on his way to work.

The next time I was to see Wayne Bethea was in a courtroom, with the prosecuting attorney asking the jury to sentence Wayne to death by hanging.

The only antidote for time inside—for men who have been in as long as Wayne—is time outside. Men in prison never get to dial a phone, tune a radio or TV—most penitentiaries censor broadcasts—or turn off a light.

Huge sums of money are spent to find a criminal, arrest him, try him, convict him, help him adjust to prison life, and then support him through years of incarceration. No money is spent to help him adjust to the free world. He is given twenty dollars or in some places as much as fifty, and sent out.

The helping hand that I had been able to extend to Wayne Bethea needed to be multiplied by a hundred. No one single person—not even I—was able to devote full time to it. Ex-convicts who were working with me had to earn a living and could only help part time. As for me, I was kept unbelievably busy trying to get official sanctions for the Seventh Step program. We now had about fifty sponsors, but they, too, could devote only spare time to helping their charges. We desperately needed some full-time help.

My efforts were beginning to pay off, though. I had obtained from the Department of Internal Revenue a non-profit status for our fledgling movement. This would give us the legal right to solicit funds on a tax-exempt basis. We had a board of directors—Judge John Royston of Kansas City, Kansas, Rue Holland, Jim Post, Jim Emerson, and me.

We were beginning to win the confidence and support of the parole officers themselves, even though we hadn't made much of an impression on their bosses on the parole board. Of course, one duty of the parole board and the officers they supervise is to help men get jobs before they get out of prison. The Kansas board had failed in that, and the reason they had is that each parole officer had a caseload of about a hundred men. The rule of thumb is that a parole officer can achieve the best possible results when handling only one man to one day of the month— that is, a total caseload of no more than thirty men at a time.

The heavy caseload is only one aspect of the problem. A parole officer's work is further complicated by the fact that the average ex-convict hates his parole officer and regards him as a policeman, a loathsome cop, a natural enemy.

This extends every interview almost endlessly. The supervisor tries to get through to the parolee, the charge tries to say as little as possible and to fool the officer who is trying to help him. One parole officer once told me it was like trying to read a letter written in invisible ink without knowing the formula for making the ink appear.

Gradually a few Kansas parole supervisors were finding out that Seventh Step men were losing their resentments, and that as these went, distrust of the parole officer went too. Seventh Step men, a few weeks out of prison and into a job, were talking freely to their supervisors, just so long as the topic of what other ex-cons were doing was avoided.

It saved time, and time is the most precious coin in the parole officer's purse. Karl Bowen, the incorrigible con, was doing so well in both his job and his attitudes, that his parole officer was using Karl to help him with his most difficult cases.

In view of the fact that there are parole regulations in every state that prohibit parolees from associating with one another, this was a giant step forward. In order to take this step, Karl's parole officer had had to get formal permission from the Kansas parole board.

A Missouri supervisor of parole officers, John Holman, arranged an invitation for me to speak to a session of the 94th Annual Congress of Correction which was going to be held in Kansas City that year.

Busy as I was, worried financially as I was, the invitation to speak to the Congress of Correction seemed just another speaking date at first reading.

Then the full meaning of the invitation began to open up before me. I was the first ex-convict ever invited to speak to the penologists and criminologists. Previous speakers included such names as J. Edgar Hoover, Lewis E. Lawes, Clinton T. Duffy, and the Attorney General and the Chief Justice of the United States.

The meeting was at the Muelbach Hotel, which is the biggest and best in Kansas City, Missouri. There were more than a thousand faces turned to me as I took the stand. They didn't seem over-friendly. I knew that John Holman had had to work hard to secure the invitation for the first ex-convict speakers to the nation's prison keepers.

Nothing to do but start. I began talking about the pre-release class at Lansing. At least that was something I knew about.

I told them of our problems, of our progress, of our successes. I told them of individual cases that I thought proved our new concept sound, and I gave them our most recent statistics. Kansas is a state where the rate of recidivism had been as high as eighty percent prior to our program. For the two hundred men in the Seventh Step program, we had a better than ninety percent success statistic. I admitted that it was a bit too early to make a full appraisal of all we were doing. I talked for an hour and twenty minutes, and ended by making a plea. "There must be scores of successful ex-convicts in each of the fifty states that you penologists represent. Use them. If you will only permit it, men like me can join with men like you and ultimately help to reduce this nation's crime bill substantially."

I sat down. Let them take it or leave it.

They took it. The audience gave me a prolonged standing ovation. And then, as the meeting ended, many of these experienced professionals crowded up to the platform to congratulate me or ask further questions.

One warden, head of a larger Eastern prison, said, "When I came in here, Mr. Sands, I thought to myself that I hadn't traveled a thousand miles to hear one more convict talk—I could get plenty of that back where I work. I was wrong, and I apologize, and want to tell you that when you are ready to extend your program to my prison, it will be welcome there."

Of course, approval of the Seventh Step idea wasn't unanimous. The Congress split into two camps, pro and anti. Perhaps I was and am prejudiced, but it seemed to me that about all the antis could say was, "Don't rock the boat, don't make waves." Apathy may be negative, but it can be powerful.

Next Monday night the class at Lansing treated me as though I'd starred in a great battle. The newspapers had reported my speech fairly, and the men knew I had not backed down on a single controversial point.

Several visiting penologists were already at Lansing to observe a class in person.

All this was exhilarating. But the wardens and other penologists who saw the class were seeing only part of the whole. Things were happening on the outside that were as heartening as the increasing sincerity of the men in the class.

R.B. Hawkins, old Arbie who had been taken out of Lansing under the sponsorship of Steve Holland, was still out. It hadn't been any kind of a Pollyanna story. You know, Steve Holland gets up, puts out his hand, and says, "I'm your friend, Arbie," and from that time on Arbie is a prominent citizen in the community—a bank director and vice-president of the local utility company.

Far from it. Steve had been unable to get Arbie a job, so he employed him himself, doing some sort of laborer's work. After awhile, Arbie quit the job, just didn't show up for work— and he didn't pay Steve back the money lent him, though the Holland Construction Company had been paying Arbie every week.

This was a violation of the whole sponsorship idea. The men sponsored were to be backed for a few hundred dollars, and then the money was to be paid back, so the sponsor would have, in effect, a revolving fund through which man after man could be paroled.

The money didn't mean an awful lot to Steve. But the principle did. He hunted Arbie down and literally picked him up by the neck, which was no trouble for Steve, but plenty for Arbie. Steve must outweigh the little guy by two hundred pounds. Steve just plain terrified Arbie into coming back to work. Then he deducted a few bucks a week from Arbie's salary until the money was paid back. After he'd taken care of that, he continued to ride herd on Arbie Hawkins till Arbie got in the habit of showing up for work and paying his bills.

There is an important point here. There are men in crime, in prison or headed there, who are merely the victims of habit. They are not very bright, and once they get used to doing something, they continue to do it. When on the take, they rob or steal or pick pockets—whatever crime they started out committing—when they want money. Broken of taking, they go to work when it is time in the morning, work till they are used to quitting in the evening, pay their bills when they are due.

These are not our most promising and desirable citizens of course. They are not the material that society wants most, not captains of industry, generals, university presidents. But they are not infringing on the rights of others, and they are not costing the public the price of their support in prison.

Arbie, for instance, is now working for a company not owned by the Hollands. He lives in a poor part of town, though he could afford to live in a better neighborhood. His reason for living in a slum is that he has always lived in a slum. But he's earning his own way and enjoying self-respect.

Perhaps this is why most reformers fail and Seventh Step succeeds. As long as a man stays free and law-abiding, we do not plague him. We do not tell him that now that he has gone up the first rung, from criminal to noncriminal, he must try for the second, such as higher education. It takes Seven Steps to make that first rung, and it is the main thing we care about. After that we motivate, but we do not dictate.

Another man Seventh Step sponsorship got out of Lansing was Pegleg Gray, a man who had lost his leg in a scrap inside. He had been walking on a peg made in the prison woodworking shop since then. He had been in twenty-seven years, he told me, when he applied to get on the list for sponsorship. I asked him, "What did you do, set fire to your mother?"

"No," he said. "I killed her with an ax."

I gave him a quick look. He wasn't smiling. I said, "Okay. We'll put you on the list."

"On the level, I held up a couple of stores and shot a policeman."

Pegleg's sponsor was none other than Joe Wallace, who was the very first ex-convict the state accepted as a sponsor. Getting Peg out of prison was only half the reward as far as I was concerned. What pleased me most was the fact that even though Joe had found it necessary to give up attending Seventh Step classes, he had chosen to help the man who most needed help.

Peg had never seen a supermarket, a car with its gear shift on the wheel—not to mention one with automatic transmission—a bank with a drive-in window. Pants had buttons instead of zippers when he last walked the streets, and every suit had a vest. Frozen food was unheard of.

Joe and his wife took Peg into their home and kept him three months, supporting him, urging him to take it easy. After twenty-seven years behind the walls, a fellow has to take freedom in very small doses. The people on the street looked different from the way they looked when he went away.

The first job that Peg got is the one he still has. He works in a macaroni factory, sitting at a table. He isn't making macaroni or being a night watchman, he's just performing some checking job, necessary but monotonous.

Pegleg doesn't care. He's paid Joe back, he's bought himself a professionally made leg, he has his own apartment, and he owns and drives a car. Pegleg is a case of a man who was well ready to change. But what chance did he have of maintaining himself on the outside? What hope of staying out could he realistically have? A devoted sponsor and his wife changed all that.

Graveyard was an interesting one too. He was a professional killer, a paid gun. You don't find many men from the Mafia and its syndicate in state prisons. I can think of only one other.

I don't think I ever knew Graveyard's real name. In any event, it doesn't matter. He looked like a Graveyard—tall, thin, and gray-skinned. He had eyes that glowed with fever and were dull with complete disinterest, all at one time. By coincidence, I never met Graveyard in Lansing. He was in the infirmary when I was out there, and someone else was taking the class when he came out of the infirmary.

The trouble that made Graveyard so gaunt was cancer of the lungs. He was dying, so the authorities released him.

No matter how sick a convict is, he always wants to die on the outside. With the help of the newspapers, we once sprang a man ninety-seven years old, who had been in forty-seven years for stealing chickens. He had been committed on an old habitual-criminal law.

But Graveyard wasn't nearly that old. He was just dying.

At an outside meeting of ex-convicts, I happened to mention one of my creditors who was really giving Pony a bad time. Jokingly I said, "It's too bad I'm rehabilitated. I'd like to bump that guy." Graveyard heard me and evidently didn't know I was joking.

The next day, in downtown Kansas City, this walking scarecrow came up to me, and said, "I'm Graveyard, Bill."

I'd heard of him. We shook hands.

"Heard you last night," he said. "Where does this guy live you want bumped?"

It took me a few minutes to figure out what he meant. I didn't know what to say.

"Look, Bill," Graveyard said, "I'm going to die. I'm a good con, and I know how much you are helping all us cons. Well, I'd like to help you. So when you find out where this guy is you want bumped, you let old Graveyard know. It will be very professional, just an accident, and this guy will be gone from the scene."

"Graveyard," I said, "when I stake this man out, you'll be the first to know."

"Anytime, Bill."

There was a man with me at the time who styled himself a preacher. I think he was a little shocked. I explained to him that Graveyard had only a few weeks to live, and that he was bringing me the only thing he had to give. I simply couldn't throw it back in his face.

Just before Graveyard died, I saw him once again. "Bill," he said, "you aren't ever going to call on me, are you?"

"No, Graveyard, I don't believe in handling things that way."

He studied me, then nodded his head, and said, "I see."

Karl Bowen had been out several months by then. The steel mill had talked about putting on twenty Lansing men if Karl made good. They had actually hired more than that, though not all at one time. Some of the men they hired didn't work out. Most did. We were pleased when the employment manager said our batting average was better than that of the average employment service.

Of course, not all our cons were as solid as Karl Bowen, and not all of them adjusted to the sponsorship program without trouble. But the more experienced sponsors, like Rue Holland, learned how to handle them pretty well. Rue had a man out under his sponsorship once, and the man called him and said that if he didn't get thirty dollars he was going to go out and hold up a store.

Rue's answer should be printed and hung on every sponsor's wall. "If your freedom isn't worth thirty dollars to you, it sure isn't to me." With which he hung up.

The con called him back, "I thought you were supposed to keep me out of prison."

Rue said, "I'm not supposed to buy it for you." Then he hung up again.

The third time the sponsored man called he said, "Well, I'm hungry and I need groceries."

Rue asked, "Where are you?"

The man said, "Home."

So Rue got up, took his car out, and drove across town to the man's efficiency apartment. Rue just walked in, went right to the refrigerator, opened it, and disclosed a very nice stock of edibles. Then he slammed the door shut, and waited, never saying a word.

The man he sponsored said, "I just wanted to see if I could con you."

Rue turned and walked out. The sponsorship worked. The man stayed out.

Another of our sponsors wasn't so smart. The con he took out was a man who had been in for more than ten years straight.

The man's name was Johnny Brandt. Dale, the sponsor, took Johnny into his home, got him a guest card at the country club, bought him imported silk-and-cashmere suits. He urged him to start living on a level of life that Johnny hadn't enjoyed ever in his free life. Johnny went to pieces. He took to drinking, turned down job offers as being beneath him, began to believe that the world, in some way, owed him the right to live like an unemployed millionaire.

We stepped in in time. I managed to get Johnny Brandt a middle-income job, white-collar work but plenty of it, and we put him under another sponsor, with a more realistic viewpoint. He did all right, but it was a close thing.

Most of our failures—not all but most—came because we did not have anyplace for the men to meet in—except for the little half of a house where Pony and I lived. We needed a clubhouse. Men on parole can be violated and sent back in if they meet each other in bars or restaurants or other public places. We badly needed a place exempt from that rule.

I had been out of town, trying to raise the money by speaking to service clubs and similar groups, and when I came back, Jim Emerson met me at the plane. His face was grooved by trouble.

"Let me have it," I said.

"Wayne," he said. "Little Wayne, the bellboy." That was the man Pony and I had set up all night with, trying to give him the courage to go to work at the hotel in the morning.

"What's he done?"

Jim sighed. "He's violated, and he is on trial for rape and robbery. They are asking the death penalty."

I've never been kicked in the pit of the belly by a mule, but I know how it feels. I learned right then.

It was an open-and-shut case. The trial was quick, and Wayne and his partner in crime were sentenced to life without possibility of parole.

It was hard to reconcile my memory of the shrinking small-framed man, who had almost scrubbed through a wall, with rape or any other kind of violence. But it was true.

As we drove into town, Jim told me the rest.

Wayne had phoned me and phoned me, but I was out of town. He had told people if he didn't find me, or some other ex-con to talk to, he was going to go out of his head. Jim Emerson and Chaplain Jim Post had both tried to talk to him. And he had listened. But then he'd answer that they just didn't understand.

So an innocent girl was raped, and Wayne's freedom was lost. We could accept one defeat. But we knew the same kind of thing would happen over and over again. That we could not accept. But I had no solution.

Chapter 13

Sometime in mid-September the bound, dust-jacketed first copy of *My Shadow Ran Fast* reached us. Pony and I went out of our heads.

All day and far into the night we rode around showing the book to everyone who had helped us. The Hollands and the Thompsons, of course, as well as every merchant who had been patient about our bills, every sponsor who had helped a man out of Lansing. To just about everybody we knew, to be honest.

I was about to know a great many more people. The publishers wanted me to go on a nationwide promotion tour.

When they agreed to pay my expenses, I took off. Cleveland was first. In the next sixty days I made more than two hundred separate appearances. On two occasions I made more than ten appearances a day. I appeared on national television, local television, local radio, and national radio.

I was interviewed by newspapers and magazines, spoke at luncheons and dinners. In Los Angeles I did twenty-three different shows in two days. It was as rough as anything I've ever gone through.

But the roughness wasn't the problem. The problem was that Pony and I had been living for months on the promise of the book royalties. And now the time we'd eagerly awaited had come—and the money wasn't coming in. Sure the book was selling. But not enough. At this rate there would be only a few thousand to spread among my creditors. I was disappointed and heartbroken.

Yes, I was doing the work I wanted to be doing. I was spreading the word about the Seventh Step, and using every bit of this chance to do it. But how was I to make a living for my family if my book didn't sell?

There was one more trip scheduled. To Chicago. When it was over, I promised myself, I would have to seriously consider the insurance job—still miraculously open. If I took the job, I would do what I could about the Seventh Step in my spare time. I would not, could not, quit the program, but we had to eat.

My rationale for being able to take a job now was one man—Ezra Kingsley. All the time I was on the road he had written me two or three times a week.

I got the letters out and reread passages I had marked.

The inmate in today's prison feels cut off from the large forces that determine his future. This leads to apathy and indifference; but we are finding a way, Bill, to peel off the layers of hardened artificialities that separate him from his real self. We have found a way to show these cons that a thinking and feeling man is never a helpless man.

On juvenile delinquency, he said,

> Few juveniles start out on an evening with any intent to steal. The idea usually comes up after some youngster has met a friend and they have been somewhere together. Most youngsters don't want to steal and neither boy would do so by himself. But neither do they want to be called chicken so they go ahead and break into some place. After they have successfully robbed a couple of places and gotten over the initial fear and built up a little nerve, then they start thinking seriously of crime and eventually get a set of tools or a pistol.
>
> Most men who have been released from prison and who have been members of our class have lived and grown up in the slums. If the community will accept these men, these cons, and show them that they are needed, they will use their unique abilities to keep a lot of youngsters from fouling up and following in their footsteps.
>
> When most professional caseworkers work on one of these kids they see nothing but a black leather jacket, a loud mouth, and a switchblade knife belonging to a foul-mouth young hoodlum. When I see one of these kids, I see a bitter, uncared-for, unloved, scared kid, putting on his act for attention. I see a kid who needs, not a whipping or a juvenile home, but someone who can help him carry out all of his bitterness, poison, and meanness. Me, and guys like me, can see in these kids ourselves twenty or thirty years ago, and we know the signs to look for.

Thus Ezra Kingsley, who had spent some of every year since his ninth behind bars, who had, according to his own account, committed every crime in the book except the sex crimes.

Don't tell me there isn't a Power working.

And then the Power worked in me. I talked to Pony first. Then I got together with Chaplain Jim Post, Jim Emerson, and Rue Holland. I was pretty embarrassed by what I had to tell them, but I wanted witnesses to back me up and to keep me from going back on the promise I was making to myself—and to the Power.

What I said—and I kept putting it in different forms, trying to ease my self-consciousness—was "If some higher power will help me achieve my goal, will save the program, I will never again lose faith or fail to declare that faith."

Rue, a staunch Catholic, was all smiles when he said, "Why don't you just say God, Bill. Make your promise to Him."

"If it'll make you happy, Rue, I will. But I'm still going to spell it G-o-o-d."

Tears stood in Jim Post's eyes as he stuck out his hand, and said, "Bill, that makes me happier than you can possibly know."

Jim Emerson just smiled and nodded.

I know. It sounds a little as though I were trying to strike a bargain with God or with the Power, or with fate, but I was desperate. I had lived long enough and hard enough to know that the only peace and happiness I would ever find was inextricably mixed up in the Seventh Step program. I knew with certainty that if I were forced to drop it for a while, and if it were to fail because of me, I would be thoroughly miserable the rest of my life. Which may have been selfishness. I'm just reporting the way I felt, the sheer desperation of the moment.

I approached my first exposure to national television with a great deal of worry and concern. I'm glad it was the Mike Douglas show. Mike is a highly skilled interviewer, but before that he is a very warm and genuine human being. Ten minutes of time had been allotted for me to tell my story. Mike gave me thirty. It was an auspicious beginning.

So on to Chicago. My publisher's publicity woman, Dorothy Strong, who handled the Chicago part of the tour, had arranged this stop with her usual vigor. The inevitable result was a backbreaking schedule. Radio, TV, national programs, local programs, press conferences, magazine interviews. Oh yes. There was a new one. "A business meeting" with W. Clement Stone. Naturally, I asked who Mr. Stone was.

"The head of a very big insurance company," Dorothy said. "Your publisher seems to think he might buy some of your books."

The Bill Sands temper popped up. "That's the only two-hour break in my schedule, and you want to use it up by having me sell books door to door!"

She shrugged. "The publisher thinks it's important."

In my low mood, I didn't feel that I could afford to offend anybody. Supposing this Mr. Stone bought ten books. I made ten percent on the retail price. Maybe he'd even buy twenty books. It was better than a poke in the eye with a sharp stick.

But I didn't feel very friendly as I was shown into Mr. Stone's big beautifully paneled office. W. Clement Stone is a man of medium stature, solidly put together, tanned, with black hair and a neat mustache. He was in superb physical condition and in the prime of his life. I began to thaw almost at once as the millionaire bounded from behind his desk, grabbed my hand, and shoved me toward a chair. In his booming voice he greeted me with "Bill Sands, I've read your book and it's terrific."

When you talk to him he gives the impression that you're doing him the greatest favor, that you're the most important thing in the world to him. Of course, it's salesmanship, but it is sincere and he uses it in his philanthropy too. And when salesmanship extends itself to giving as well as earning, it becomes something else. Such as love of mankind.

His questions about me and about Seventh Step were all sharp and to the point. When he had asked the things he wanted to ask, he said, "I've ordered some copies of your book to give to people who ought to read it."

"That's nice."

"Aren't you interested in how many books I bought?" Mr. Stone asked.

"Of course I am."

He smiled happily. "Ten thousand."

I goggled. Speechless Bill Sands—a rare phenomenon.

"I'm going to give them away to reform schools, prisons, boys' clubs, men in trouble, underprivileged youngsters, high schools, libraries. I'm going to put a copy of that book every place I can where someone might need its message—and you're going to help me!"

My recollection is that I said something brilliant. Like, "Huh?"

"I want to see your program extended. I don't know whether you can do more in Kansas State Prison than you have, but I'd like to see something like it started in other places. As fast as possible."

I nodded, thinking that was easier said than done. Just the Lansing program had taken the time and spare money of a lot of good businessmen, such as the Hollands.

Mr. Stone went on, "And I'm particularly interested in getting the Seventh Step message to underprivileged boys *before* they get into crime. Keep thinking of a way to do that."

"Yes, sir, I will."

He relaxed. He had made his point. Actually all he had done was to sell me on doing what I wanted to do more than anything else in the world. But it is the nature of W. Clement Stone to lavish his own enthusiasm freely, in case the person he is talking to cannot match his own enormous vitality.

He asked me to tell him more about the Lansing program. I did. I told him all about the more than two hundred parolees.

"And so far you're ninety percent successful," he mused. "I really wasn't thinking about that. I already knew it. What I meant was, how are you financing this work?"

That opened a floodgate. He heard about my debts, about the storekeepers and the Thompsons and Hollands. And I told him about my hopes for the book, which sales hadn't yet justified. I finished on a slightly more optimistic note. The business community of Kansas City was showing more interest all the time.

His reaction was startling. "You mean that you have an effective program going, and all it needs is money? Well, I have plenty of that! How much do you need?"

I gulped. I'd only been there ten minutes, had heard of W. Clement Stone the day before for the first time in my life, and here he was presumably offering to solve all my troubles.

When I could talk, I said, "A quarter of a million dollars ought to extend the program to tens of thousands of men."

Mr. Stone shrugged, as though he gave away little sums like that every day. "Get me a written proposition showing where the money will be used, and I'll see that you get it. Now, about your personal position. How much do you owe, and where?"

If this was a dream, I never wanted to wake up. I sat very still. I had already explained about my debts. Now I went into a little more detail.

Again, this man nodded. "I'll take care of that. You can't do good work when you're burdened down with money worries. Nobody can. Let's see. This is Thursday. Can you be here

Tuesday with the written forecast of what the program needs in the way of money *and* a list of your own debtors and the amount you owe them?"

"Yes, sir." Could I? I could have been there the next day. Sleep was a thing I would never need again, eating was nonessential.

My hand was pumped again, and I was in the outer office, arranging with the secretary for the Tuesday meeting.

My head was buzzing with plans. I'd get Rue Holland to come up to Chicago with me Tuesday. I'd get him and his father and his brothers to double check my forecast figures. I'd get Pony to go over the list of our personal debts, to make sure I didn't forget one. I'd . . . Suddenly I realized. The miracle I had asked the Power for had come about.

Pony took over the personal debt list, and she got a lawyer to help her. The total was twenty-one thousand dollars and a little over.

Meanwhile, Rue and Jim Post and I worked at the happy job of planning to spend a quarter of a million dollars. Two hundred and fifty thousand dollars. And last week I had been scrounging for gas money to get out of Lansing.

First and foremost, we wanted the Kansas City clubhouse and a salary for a manager. Then programs in other states. We had dozens of letters to pore over, from prison officials and parole officers and other elected officials. Some of them had heard me when I spoke before the Congress of Correction, some of them had heard about the program through TV or radio or the newspapers. Some of them were correspondents of Jim Post. Some had already read *My Shadow Ran Fast.*

Rue and I flew to Chicago. The second interview with Mr. Stone went as fast as the first. I introduced Rue at once and handed over the prospectus. Mr. Stone read it as quickly as he did everything else.

"Very good," he said, laying it down. "I'm especially pleased that you have already set up your gift tax, nonprofit corporation structure. Saves time. How about your personal debts?"

So I handed that over, too. Mr. Stone has a built-in adding machine. He grunted as he checked the total and snapped an intercom switch. "Check to Bill Sands for twenty-seven thousand five hundred."

I said, "That's a little over five thousand more than I owe."

"The rest is to cover your expenses moving to Chicago. We'll need to work closely together if we are to expand this program into other states." His logic was obvious.

"But this is personal money, not program money. How do I pay it back?"

Mr. Stone was impatient. "Your book will be a success. You'll be writing other books, giving lectures and being paid for them. You're going to be rich, Bill."

Under the force of his charm and optimism, it was hard to believe otherwise. I asked about signing a note for my personal debts. Clement Stone waved an impatient hand. "First things first. You're really doing me a favor, Bill. My money can't accomplish much for the people I want to help if there aren't men like you, the right kind of men, to use it."

Put this way, it almost sounded as though he ought to be thanking me, instead of the other way around. But I felt so full of gratitude to Mr. Stone that I wanted to keep reaching for his hand and shaking it. W. Clement Stone has no time for that sort of thing. He kept plowing ahead.

"According to your prison-program budget, you'll need five thousand dollars the first month, gradually climbing till you're spending twenty thousand a month at the end of a year and a half. That just about takes care of the full quarter of a million. Now, we'll consider this seed money. After it's gone you'll be on your own. Right?"

I could only nod.

He flipped the intercom again and ordered a second check, made out to the foundation. His staff had studied under him—the two checks were on his desk in moments. He signed them and handed them over to me.

I was goggling. "Do you mean you're putting up the whole quarter of a million yourself?"

Rue and I started muttering our thanks. We didn't get far. W. Clement Stone had done his from-behind-the-desk bounce and was escorting us to the door. We were outside before we quite understood what had been done for the Seventh Step movement—and for me personally.

Really, we were still in shock when the plane landed at Kansas City. That's one of the troubles with airline travel—you don't get time to adjust. I was adjusting to Kansas City, where I'd lived in a state of semipoverty, from Chicago, where I was the honored friend of a prince among millionaires.

Pony was at the airport to drive us home. I swept her off the ground and gave her a hug that almost broke her ribs. She got loose and gasped, "What's the matter with you?" before she could get her breath back.

I waved the two checks at her. She grabbed them and lost a little more breath. "Bill!"

Rue had to help me explain what had happened. Pony didn't seem to believe it any more than we had.

I'm afraid everything else got sort of short notice for the next week as Pony and I drove around Kansas City, paying off our patient creditors. Once again we offered to pay Mr. Arbeiter interest. This time he agreed—in a way. "Interest is for bankers, as I said once before. But I would take a free, autographed copy of Bill's book."

I ran out to the car and got a copy—somehow or other I always seemed to have one handy—and inscribed it to Mr. Arbeiter and his wife.

Les Thompson was my biggest creditor. When I handed him a check for almost eight thousand dollars, he honored it with the briefest of glances and slid it into the top drawer of his desk.

"Aren't you going to say something, Les?"

"Bill," he said, "Barbara and I never expected anything else. We had more faith in you than you had in yourself."

Rue Holland reacted just the way Les had. I don't think he even bothered to look at the amount on the check—an amount burned indelibly into my memory—$6,150. Then he said, "Thanks, Bill." I had learned my lesson with Dr. Les. I just said that he was welcome.

Chapter 14

W. Clement Stone came out to Lansing to look the program over. Ezra took advantage of Mr. Stone's visit to ask him for some books to read that would help Ezra develop his own potentialities. Mr. Stone was amused when Ezra said, "I don't think I'll ever care about making two hundred million dollars, but I have an idea that the same principles could be applied in other fields."

Rue Holland was very anxious to get Ezra out of Lansing and onto the street, where he could be more widely useful. I was somewhat dubious about it. We could certainly use Ezra in a wider field than the Kansas State Prison provided, but the new Seventh Step Foundation had not been set up as a legal aid society. Aiding an individual man out of the penitentiary could, I feared, set a dangerous precedent.

We pondered, and then decided that an individual action on my part didn't involve the foundation at all. So I agreed to testify whenever Ezra came up before the parole board. As I remember it, I think I said I'd be there if I had to crawl from coast to coast on my hands and knees. At any rate I felt that way about getting Ezra out on parole. Rue took an active part in getting together character witnesses for Ezra and seeking legal advice.

Before we could move to Chicago, I had to find a clubroom in the city for Seventh Step. Now that we had the money we didn't want any repetition of the Wayne Bethea tragedy—of a man harming innocent people and losing his freedom because of his desperate loneliness.

We found just what we needed on the second floor of an office building on Minnesota Avenue. The meeting room would hold a hundred men, and it had plenty of room for easy chairs to read or chat in, checkers, chess, and card games, for a modest library. Off to the side were smaller rooms for office space and private counseling chambers. Karl Bowen agreed to take over my job as the ex-convict in charge of the Lansing program, and with Ezra heading the committee in the prison, I was leaving the first prerelease class in good hands.

And then Joe Wallace, my first helper in the program came back to us. He was the first of many men to find out that once you start in Seventh Step work you feel lonely and only half-useful in anything else. When I asked him if he and his wife didn't still feel that his work with ex-convicts would be harmful to their child, he shook his head.

"No, Bill," he said, "we've changed our minds completely about that. Everybody who knows who you are knows you're an ex-convict and people respect you anyway. We've been talking it over and thinking about it and we finally decided that it's better for all of us, our daughter too, to be completely honest about my record. If the other kids are going to hold it against her that her dad once made a mistake we're going to have to give her enough love to make up for it. And we know we can do it. We've made up our minds that we're not going to let ourselves feel guilty and ashamed about my record. It's better to face it from the beginning—that way my daughter will never be shocked about it."

Lansing didn't really need Joe, so we decided he'd come to Chicago with us. Warden Jack Johnson was interested in trying a Seventh Step program in the big Cook County jail there, and Joe agreed to set it up.

Though it's called a jail, the lock-up for big Cook County, which included Chicago, is really more like a state prison. It has about everything that a state prison has, including its own electric chair. And, of course, Cook County has a bigger population than many states have.

I told Joe, "Initiating this program will be entirely your responsibility. I have obtained the necessary clearances for you through Warden Jack Johnson, and he has assured me that you will be given the full cooperation of his staff. When you're actually ready to open a class, call me if you need me."

Joe agreed, and I knew I could count on him.

I had opened a Chicago office and hired a perfect gem of a secretary named Vicki LaHaie. Just keeping my calendar of appearances and trying to keep my schedule straight was almost a full-time job for her.

One day, when I had just returned to the office from a lecture engagement, Vicki greeted me with, "A publicity woman named Barbara Wilkerson just called and asked me if you could go out to the airport with her right away."

"Why?" I asked.

"Chuck Percy is coming in on a plane, from Washington, and he wants to meet you." Of course I knew who Chuck Percy was. He had been the head of the Republican platform committee during the Eisenhower years, had recently been narrowly defeated for the governorship of Illinois, and was currently serving as chairman of the board of the Bell and Howell Corporation.

I knew Barbara Wilkerson, and she is a level-headed girl. So I met her and we went out to the airport.

When Percy's plane landed, he was greeted, as usual, by a number of reporters with their inevitable questions.

"What are you doing in Chicago, Mr. Percy?"

"I came here to meet and spend a couple of hours with Bill Sands," he answered.

"What are you going to talk about?"

"Problems of mutual interest," Mr. Percy replied. "Perhaps we'll have a newsworthy statement for you after we've talked."

All of this happened before I was even introduced to him. He simply pushed his way through the reporters, walked over to where I was standing with Barbara Wilkerson, stuck out his hand and said, "I'm Chuck Percy."

He looked even younger than his pictures, and his voice was surprisingly deep and resonant.

We quickly walked to the airport restaurant, where, according to Mr. Percy, he had a table set aside for us. He had about two hours to talk to me.

When we were seated, I asked, "What can I do for you?"

"You can teach me about prisons," he replied. "In my recent gubernatorial campaign, I realized that I knew very little about the field of correction. I'd like to know a lot about it. I've read your book, and I'm hoping you can help enlighten me."

Naturally I was pleased. And for the next two hours I did the best I could to inform him of the problems of penology. I tried not to editorialize, and he appreciated that fact. But the time wasn't long enough.

"Mr. Percy," I concluded, "there is simply no way that I can give you the information you want in one two-hour sitting. If you really want to know, in depth, you will have to go inside a prison and talk to men who are serving time. You can't afford to spend your time talking to the men the average warden will select for you. The man you want to know is the hard-core convict who will level with you and tell you what it's really like. You should also talk to men who are on parole or recently discharged. It's the only way you can learn the truth. And it's more easily said than done. In most prisons you'd have access to, you would see only what the authorities want you to see. And you would be sure to end up with a distorted view."

"Go on," he said.

"If you will let me arrange it I can take you into the Kansas State Prison at Lansing. Because of the work I've been doing there, I can see to it that you talk to a representative cross-section of the inmate population. I would like you to visit one of our prerelease classes and to talk with some of our graduates on the outside. But there's one catch."

"What's that?"

"Kansas is a Republican state, and you are one of the most prominent Republicans in the country. It will be difficult for you to visit that state without publicity or political hoopla. But if you come in with a lot of fanfare, the guys in the joint will figure it's all a shuck with you. Those cons will think that you're just using them to further your own political ambitions. They will figure that if you were really sincere you'd come into the state very quietly and leave the same way."

Percy made no comment, but he took his calendar from his brief case and studied it intently. "It's going to be very difficult to find time," he said. "Every day for the next two months is solid with appointments. The only days I have free are one Sunday and Monday that I have set aside for my family."

"That would be perfect, Mr. Percy," I said. "It so happens our classes are on Monday night. If you could spend those two days with us you would have a deeper insight into the problems of convicts than you could possibly gain otherwise through months of study."

"Let me call you," he said. "I'll see what I can arrange. Don't count on it."

Our time was over, and we shook hands and parted. The waiting reporters were disappointed. Percy issued no statement. It had been a very interesting conversation, but I didn't seriously expect that I would ever hear from Chuck Percy again. He called the next day. He wanted to visit Lansing over his one free weekend, and he asked me to arrange it.

I made plans for his visit in what I'm afraid was a somewhat skeptical spirit. But when the time came, I found he was as good as his word. I don't know how he did it, but when his plane landed in Kansas City, there wasn't a reporter in sight.

On those two days he spent in Lansing, he worked as hard as I have ever seen any man work. He gave himself up to us for as long as eighteen hours each day, and concentrated on listening to the men, observing the conditions of their lives, and absorbing the feel of the prison. Every single convict or ex-convict who talked to him was completely captivated. On Monday night he spoke before the prerelease class. He is one of the few squarejohns we have ever invited to speak there, and he is also one of the few who really could reach the men. He told about the struggles his family had had when he was a boy, during the Depression, and he leveled with them about what his recent defeat at the polls had meant to him. He said it hurt—and tried to explain how it had helped him, too. He thought it had saved him from the danger of overconfidence. I don't suppose the convicts exactly identified with him, but they certainly heard him, and they liked what they heard.

After his visit to Lansing, Percy continued to show a lively interest in the Seventh Step program. He joined us as a member of the National Advisory Board.

When I got back to Chicago after Chuck Percy's visit to Lansing, Joe Wallace telephoned to say he was about ready to go with the Cook County program.

"Now I need your help," he said. "I have my committee selected and partially trained. Before I actually start the pre-release classes, I'd like to do something really big for the entire jail population. Sort of as an advertisement for our program."

"What do you have in mind?"

"I'd like to get some top entertainers to do a show, under our auspices, in the Main Yard. What I'd like is if you would get some prominent people there. Like Mr. Percy and Mr. Stone. It would impress the guys in the joint. It will help me kick off the program."

Since my own years in show business, I have been fortunate in being able to call friends and some of the finest performers in the business. I have great affection for all show business people, but two of the ones I love most are Phil Ford and Mimi Hines. When Phil and Mimi heard what Joe was planning for the Cook County jail, they didn't even wait to be asked if they'd give us a hand—they volunteered.

When the show began, there were twenty-five hundred inmates assembled in the big Main Yard. For security's sake,

the most desperate two hundred men in the jail—men awaiting sentence for felonies, on trial for murder, or men condemned to the electric chair—were held in a special section
right in front of the platform. I couldn't help but think that it
was a heavy price to pay for a reserved seat.

There I was as an MC again, introducing Mr. Stone, Mr.
Percy, and, finally, Phil and Mimi. The jail had television facil-
ities, so all the men were familiar with Ford & Hines. They
got off with a good hand. And then they just about killed
themselves for more than an hour to put on a show that was
unusually great—even for them.

When they finished, the men kept shouting for more. I
took the mike again and said, "Phil and Mimi came here as
good friends of mine. Now they're friends of yours too. So
you'll be glad to know that Mimi has just signed to replace
Barbra Streisand as the lead in the great Broadway show,
Funny Girl. Mimi, will you sing 'People' for us?"

Phil sat at the piano and played the introduction to that
great song. You probably remember it—the words are about
the need of people for other people. Trailing the mike cord,
Mimi stepped down from the platform and sat on the Main
Yard lawn, completely surrounded by the two hundred
reserved-seat felons.

As Mimi sang, sitting there small and alone among those
desperate men, I watched the faces in the audience. Her innocent faith, coupled with the touching lyric she was singing,
worked a transformation in even the most cynical of her hear-
ers. When she finished, the applause I had expected didn't
come. She rose and walked slowly back toward the crude out-
door stage in a complete silence. Just as she reached the platform, the men, still silent, came to their feet. The stillness was
suddenly broken by the harsh rattling sound of the machine-

gun ratchets, as the gun-tower guards instinctively swiveled their weapons toward the mass movement.

A second later the applause hit. The men stood in their places, clapping and cheering and whistling, until Mimi had been escorted from the Yard.

My publishers decided that *My Shadow Ran Fast* deserved another promotional tour, along the West Coast. The book was selling, but not spectacularly. I dreaded another of those grinds, but I agreed with Mr. Stone that *My Shadow* was the most valuable tool we had for spreading the Seventh Step doctrines. So I hit the TV-radio-interview-luncheon-dinner trail again. It was almost as lethal as the first tour. Once I did twenty-five separate appearances in two-and-a-half days.

On this trip I appeared with Art Linkletter for the first time. He took me through a twenty-one-minute interview with such skill and dexterity that the time was just nothing. Afterward Art told me that I had received more time than anyone in the history of his *House Party*—the previous record—eighteen minutes—was held by Cecil B. DeMille.

Another entertainer went all out to help me—Tennessee Ernie Ford omitted the hymn he usually includes in his program in favor of a talk by me about the plight of ex-convicts.

Linkletter told me to tell my publisher to start printing more books. "I pitched your book harder than I have ever tried to sell any person or product in all my years, and your publishers know what kind of salesman I am."

Art was certainly right. Within three days of my appearance on his show, three wonderful things happened. I received over two thousand letters from his audience. Every book wholesaler in the country was out of stock on *My Shadow Ran Fast*. And the best was to come—*My Shadow* got its first mention on the nonfiction best seller list!

Back in Chicago, Warden Jack Johnson of the Cook County jail asked me if I would speak at a fund-raising dinner for the Chicago Better Boys Foundation, of which he was a director. Of course I said I would.

Jack Johnson is, after all, a giant among modern penologists. A thoroughly compassionate man, he is also thoroughly skilled and educated in the curious knowledge that goes to make up the world of a modern warden.

Warden Johnson's arrangements for the affair were bizarre but effective. The dinner was at the jail instead of at a hotel. The invitations were in the form of warrants of arrest, and police cars picked up the guests. And the guests were received at the jail as though they had really been pinched—they were mugged, finger-printed, and given a number.

Then they were taken on a complete tour of the jail, including the deathhouse. Warden Johnson couldn't show them Death Row because he had abolished it—he kept his condemned prisoners integrated with the general prison population. Dinner was in the mess hall, and it was straight prison fare—the beans and bologna that, in all too many jails and penitentiaries, are a steady diet because they impose a minimum of strain on the kitchen staff and mess budget.

The guests had been hand-picked. Three of them joined the tour of the jail after the others had been brought in by the police cars. The three were dressed as well as the successful business and professional men who were the other guests. But the clothes were only donned for the evening—the normal garb of these three "guests" would be prison denim. They were all awaiting execution.

In order to complete the disguise, Pony was with one of them, posing as his wife. Barbara Wilkerson accompanied another. And Bill Truesdale, a local investment broker, was with the third, acting as though they were business associates.

When I got up to start my job as MC, I was full of confidence. Warden Johnson hoped to raise fifteen thousand dollars at the dinner, and Clement Stone, with whom I had come, told me he was going to start the ball rolling with a five-thousand-dollar check. Anyone who's ever presided over a fund-raising rally will tell you that a kickoff like that makes the whole job simple.

Nevertheless, I built my pitch carefully, talking about the three steps society can take against crime. It can lock a man up. Or it can try to reform him while he's locked up. Or it can take the third step—which is to try and reach him when he is still a boy, before he commits his first crime. (Of course, this had nothing to do with the Seven Steps of our own program, but my mind was running in a rhythm of steps.)

I ended up by congratulating the men present on their successful lives and enviable reputations. But, I wondered, was there anyone present who would have had a happier life if something in his youth hadn't happened? Or who would like to confess some youthful error in order to sleep better than night? The question was a shock. The guests had come to learn more about their unfortunate fellow Chicagoans and to contribute to a worthwhile movement. They had not expected to be asked to participate in an evangelical confession session.

But a thin ascetic-looking man wearing a handsome silk suit stood up and gravely said, "I know I would sleep easier tonight if I had been reached when I was a kid."

He stood steadily under the eyes of all his fellow-diners—which was no easy thing to do. I asked him to give his name and occupation.

"My name is Bill Witherspoon," he said. "And in nineteen days I will die in the electric chair."

Everybody in the room seemed to share in the gasp that went up. I know I gasped, and I knew what was coming. Bill was the man who had squired Pony to the dinner.

When the hall was absolutely quiet, I said that there were two more condemned men among us. Then I asked all three to come up to the platform.

"Ladies and gentlemen," I said, "these men are not asked to come up as objects of our curiosity. They are examples of exactly what the Better Boys Foundation is trying to prevent. I'm going to ask each of them to tell you about *his* boyhood."

It must have been terribly hard for those three men, living so close to death, to retrace the path that had taken them there. But each one went through with it. It was only toward the end—when they tried to ask, to hope, that no other boy would ever have to confront the grim fate which they themselves now faced—that first one, and the other two, broke down.

Turning directly to the audience, I took the microphone back and said, "Ladies and gentlemen, from the moment these three men passed the point of no return in their lives, they have not heard a single kind word from any source. The policemen who questioned them, the judge who sentenced them, and the newsmen who wrote about their crimes, have all heaped verbal abuse on their shoulders. I do not say it was not deserved. I do say that tonight they deserve something better.

"You people shared a dinner with three men condemned to die. You have heard them tell their stories—and you can understand how painful it was for them—with the hope that they could help prevent some kid from following in their tragic footsteps. I would like these three men to return to their cells tonight with a sound of approval for once ringing in their ears. Tonight I think they have earned that. Do you agree?"

The ovation that greeted my question far surpassed what even I had expected. It was so warm that the three men, so soon to die, broke down and cried openly. So did many of the sophisticated successful men in the audience.

What I did next wasn't pleasant, and it isn't pleasant to remember. But where brutality is concerned, nothing is pleasant. For the sake of the three condemned men, and for the sake of dozens or perhaps hundreds of boys not yet condemned, I had to tell it like it is.

I called up the man who had been Pony's escort and put my arm around his shoulders. "This man is scheduled to be the first of the three to go. None of you know him well, yet you have eaten a dinner with him and shared a moment in which he bared his soul because he wanted to do some good for somebody else. For that, you applauded him. Do you know what comes after the applause? I'll tell you what will happen if somebody doesn't do something to stop it—Bill Witherspoon will be strapped in that electric chair, just nineteen days from now. When the current tears through his body, he's going to strain against the straps in convulsions. His tongue will turn black. The smell of his burning flesh will permeate the execution chamber. A black hood tied over his head will be the only reason the witnesses won't see his eyes pop from their sockets.

"Now, ladies and gentlemen of Chicago . . . You, who are good and honest citizens, which one of you will step up to the panel and push the button? It is your electric chair, not the warden's. If these men die in this way, it is your responsibility."

While the audience absorbed what I had said, the prison guards entered the room, surrounded the three doomed men who had dined with us, and led them away. When they had gone, I made my plea for the Better Boys Foundation. I said quietly that there were boys—young boys, small boys—out on the streets of Chicago at that very moment who were sure to end up awaiting execution in this very jail. Unless someone cared, that is.

Clement Stone was reaching for his checkbook, but other men beat him to the draw. Warden Johnson, who had hoped for fifteen thousand dollars, got more than four times that much for his foundation.

As this is written, the three men who spoke at that dinner are still alive. But any or all of them may die before this book can be published—their sentences have not been commuted. If they die they will die needlessly. Capital punishment has never deterred anyone. When it was the penalty for pickpocketing in England, the pickpockets are said to have apparently rejoiced. After all a public hanging drew great crowds—among them the pickpockets plied their trade more successfully than on any other occasion.

Chapter 15

A great many of our convicts plan to work with delinquent kids when they get out—to help the youngsters, of course, and also as a means of helping themselves. A man who knows he is looked up to and depended upon by several teenagers is very unlikely to take a false step that heads him back behind bars.

The most important thing to do for juvenile criminals is to change them before they are confined with a bunch of their contemporaries. Reform schools, juvenile houses of detention, even juvenile forestry camps, are often schools for criminal technique.

When I went to reform school I didn't have the vaguest idea of how anyone went about blowing a safe. When I came out I not only knew several techniques for getting inside a box, but I had memorized lists of where safes of different kinds were located, how much money they held at different times, when they were watched and when they weren't.

Up till then I had been more or less confined to sticking up Mom-and-Pop grocery stores. Now I was a graduate criminal. I could hope to make some big money. Certain boys in a reform school sometimes will know more about the money habits of the large chains—filling stations, supermarkets, and so on—than some of the executives in the home offices of the companies know.

A little thought makes it apparent that the one thing that boys in a reform school have in common besides sex (which all boys have in common) is crime. They come from all sorts of backgrounds, all ethnic groups, all the localities in the state— big cities, crossroad towns, ranches, farms. So they talk about crime—how to commit different crimes, which ones pay best, how to set up an alibi, how to talk to cops. And—if they didn't know before they came there—they learn to hate. And they want to get even.

Even sex is not so common a topic in reform schools as crime and how to commit it. The strength of the drive toward women varies in each boy. Some will mature into homosexuality—possibly a larger number of them will because they have been exposed to it in institutions which deprived them of girls' companionship.

And their backgrounds, as I said, are of all kinds. It is a mistake to think that only slums produce juvenile delinquency. According to J. Edgar Hoover, one out of four males under eighteen in the middle-class suburbs might someday make it to a police blotter.

On a lighter note, I remember a speech I was paid to make in a little town in Kansas. This was a place with a population of thirty-nine hundred. They not only paid me a good fee but also covered my expenses from California and back to the Coast. They were scared, and they felt they needed my help badly. Every adult in town must have been there to hear me—sixteen hundred people. After speaking to them, I was to go out to the high school and speak to their kids.

They had trouble, the mayor told me. At a high-school dance three of the boys had got drunk—then two of them got into a fight and broke some windows in the high-school gym.

I couldn't laugh. The problem was real to them, but all I could think of was Meredith Willson's song about trouble in River City—kids buckling their knickers below the knee instead of above, shooting pool instead of billiards, and saying "So's your old man."

It wasn't a laughing matter to them. I hope I helped the kids at the school, but I told the parents' meeting—the one with the sixteen hundred adults at it—that they ought to count themselves lucky to be raising their children where they were. That in New York there were neighborhoods where you had to cut someone or hold up a store or terrorize a subway car before you could be admitted to a gang.

That was a real pleasure, talking to such nice people.

Another pleasure was finding out that what I'd thought was one of my saddest and most inexplicable failures had not been that at all.

While I was still writing *My Shadow*, I met a boy called Ricky. He was one of the finest-looking boys I've ever seen—six feet one, a hundred and ninety pounds, marvelous teeth, dark hair, sparkling eyes. Ricky looks like movie stars wish they did, and he's bright as well. Bright? He tests out genius grade.

When I met him, he was in prison, at the early stages of J.D.—stealing hubcaps and credit cards for free gas. He was so much the sort of youngster this country needs that I spent more time with him than I could afford. After his release I took him home with me and talked over his problems with him. I borrowed a racing car and took him riding in it, taught him to corner and let him drive it. I also took him flying. I did all this to show him what a legitimate thrill was like, that there were better and more exciting things than breaking the law.

As I became better acquainted with Ricky, I learned that his basic problem was disappointment with his parents. His father was a nice guy but a weakling, and his mother, a vain, selfish woman, dominated the family. Her most obvious interest in her son was her hope that his athletic success and his popularity would help her move up the social ladder. Once, when a baseball umpire called Ricky out on a narrow tag, she hurried out to the parking lot, got into her car, and repeatedly rammed the umpire's car with it.

Ricky and I talked over his problems, and I recall telling him—in front of his parents—that I understood exactly what was wrong. He wanted his father to be strong and he wasn't; he wanted his mother to be a saint and instead she was a jerk.

Then I said: "Ricky, you can love your mother because she is your mother. She has done what she thinks is right for you, as she sees it. But you must face the fact that she's a jerk, and love her with that in mind."

I didn't win any popularity contest with the parents, but I thought I got through to Ricky. He agreed with me that he had been seeking thrills strictly in doing something wrong, and seemed to agree that this was a sucker's game. I believed that he was through with it.

And then I learned that he was in custody down in Texas for stealing a car and driving it across a state line. This was a blow. I tried to forget it as I went on working with other guys and other kids, but I couldn't. Finally, I wrote about it in my book in the hope that I might still reach Ricky or, if that failed, at least reach some other kid who was thinking the same way.

Long after *My Shadow* came out, but while I was still living
in Kansas City, Ricky phoned me. He was out, and he wanted
to come to see me. Would I have time to spare for him?

Would I! He came over that same night, and I have never
been more pleased to see anyone. When he walked in, I
remember I was thinking that at least I would have this one
more chance to straighten him out. But I was wrong—he
didn't need it. He had straightened himself out in a jail cell in
Texas after he was picked up.

The beef they got him on was a minor one, little more
than joyriding really. And if he had not been with a couple
of other kids he might not have been mixed up in anything.
They hadn't damaged the car they had taken, and the Texas
authorities were not anxious to jail them because the owner of
the car lived in another state. Crossing the state line made it a
federal offense, but the federal courts weren't too upset about
it either. Finally the police offered to release the boys, provided
that their parents came in to pay their fines and pick them up.
The two other boys agreed to phone their parents, but Ricky
had been doing some thinking. When it came to his turn to
call his family, he said: "I talked to Bill Sands not long ago,
and he said a solid man learns to ride his own beefs. Well, I
intend to be solid, and this is my beef, not my folks. I stole the
car, they didn't."

So he refused to call his parents. And he pleaded guilty to
the charges against him.

He started serving his time in the federal installation at
Englewood, Colorado, which is a youth and juvenile institution. The youngsters there are taught the usual high-school
courses and play in a league with regular high schools. In nine
months Ricky finished the two years of school he had missed,
broke a state track record, led the school baseball team in bat-

ting, was outstanding as a football player and won a wrestling championship. The athletic director must have cried when they transferred Ricky to the Federal Prison Camp at Tucson just before his release.

He had earned admission to a good university on his athletic and scholastic record, and everything looked fine. Then, only three days before his release, he was in trouble again. Airmail stamps were found on him, and at Tucson—as in most penal institutions—stamps are contraband. The authorities knew that they weren't his stamps, because he was going out in three days and did not need them. So obviously he was carrying them from one inmate to another.

They offered to forget the whole thing if Ricky would name the other boys. He refused. They threatened to revoke his parole, and he said, "In that case, I'll just do some more studying." So he served another six months before being released.

It was then that he came to see me. He had read my book, and when he saw I was worrying about him, he wanted to let me know it was okay. He was really staying out of trouble this time. He has too. First, he enrolled in a junior college and arranged to go to the college of his choice when the semester changed. Then, all on his own, he took a job heaving beer barrels to keep himself in shape.

Since then he has transferred to his college and returned home to his parents, supporting himself by selling Fuller Brushes in the summer. Of course he does well at it—makes as much as two or three hundred dollars a week. Incidentally, he recently told me that I had misjudged his mother.

"She does an awful lot of dumb things, Bill, but she doesn't mean anything wrong by them. I'm getting along fine with her. Basically she's a pretty nice person."

I didn't argue. But if I had tried to tell him that in the first place, would he have listened?

Ricky, of course, is from what is essentially a good home. Not all the kids we meet in our Seventh Step work have so much going for them, and not all of them can be reached by talk, however down to earth. I remember one youngster from a Chicago slum who needed another kind of treatment. I met him one day while doing some work with the boys' club there, with Karl Bowen helping me. I had a full day's interviews scheduled when the club secretary brought me a message. They had dragged in a teenage gang-leader against his will, and he was in the anteroom, where he was telling everyone he didn't believe that I would dare talk to him. Well, I couldn't disappoint the boys lining up to see me, but I thought I couldn't avoid having a look at this youngster either, so between interviews I excused myself to the boys waiting and promised them I'd be right back.

In the next room I found as tough a youngster as I'd ever seen, bristling with resentment and all ready for a fight, with his hand on a bicycle chain hanging out of his jacket. Before he could open his mouth, I apologized for not being able to spend much time with him myself and explained that I had a helper who would be glad to see him. Very briefly, I told him about the time Karl had done in Lansing, carefully emphasizing the toughest parts—the beatings and the tear-gassing and the time in solitary—and adding that Karl was interested in seeing that no kid should go through what he had gone through before he gave up taking. But I saw the youngster's lip curling in a sneer as I left him without giving him time to reply, let alone to drag out his bicycle chain.

I told Karl what I had let him in for, and he headed for the anteroom. He is not very big physically, and perhaps for this reason the kid thought, "This is someone I can take." So he reached into his jacket and got a grip on the bicycle chain. Without a second's hesitation Karl strode across the room and socked the boy so hard on the jaw that he went sailing up against the wall. Then, without raising his voice, Karl told him, "If you take that chain out, I'm going to take it away from you and break both your legs."

He meant it. Luckily for the boy, he realized that he had made a mistake. The talk that followed straightened him out, and further made him a staunch supporter of everything Karl was doing. At that time Karl was working on a program in the Cook County jail, and the boy went with him and trailed after him like a puppy, hoping to find some way he could help. He and his gang were never in trouble with the authorities again.

Karl's approach on this occasion was hardly that of a normal counseling session, but it worked—and that's what we care about. There are kids—lots of kids—who just can't identify with someone unless they first discover that the guy is tougher than they are.

Knowing this, I have, in speaking around the country, developed a technique for high schools that differs from the speeches I give to adults. And I've even worked up a sub-technique for *really* tough schools—unlike the one in Kansas with broken gym windows.

Sometimes I stand on the platform and say that someplace in the school there may be a gang of kids carrying knives or perhaps bicycle chains, who wear their hair too long, or too short, who sport distinctive jackets, probably leather. In other words, I describe a typical movie-imitating high-school gang. The description goes on until heads start to turn in the audience, showing me where the gang is sitting. (They always sit together.) Then I address them directly.

I begin by telling them that I don't think they are tough, that stealing parts off cars or robbing eighty-year-old men of three dollars and ninety-five cents has nothing to do with toughness.

"In any prison I've ever seen, guys like you could be made into punks in their first twenty minutes in Main Yard. And if you don't know what a punk is, I'll tell you."

And I do, making it just as brutal and disgusting as I dare. Finally I take out my money clip, flash it, count the bills in it, saying: "My car is in the parking lot, and I shall be walking to it alone. Why don't you big-shots try making a real scene. Why not take this clip away from me?"

There is more, but that's enough to give the general picture. The idea, of course, is to make the other kids laugh at the gang instead of standing in awe of them. One good schoolwide laugh, and a gang like that breaks up.

Once, in a suburb of Chicago, my bluff was called—only it wasn't a bluff. I meant it. When I stepped out into the parking lot, about a half-dozen of them were standing by the driver's side of my car. I looked back and saw the entire student body of that school at the windows. Had the building been a boat, it would have tipped over!

There was nothing to do but walk toward the surely, sneering group, telling myself as I went that they did not really want to get me. The smart way would have been prison-style—in the back as I went down a crowded corridor. There wasn't much comfort in the thought, but I had to walk straight and slowly toward my car. If I faltered, all the good my speech had done would be worse than wasted.

As I walked, I was trying to decide which of the boys was the head. Every mob, every gang or goon squad, has a head. Cut it off and the rest scatter. I settled on a boy in the middle, because the eyes of his neighbors flickered toward him to see what he would do, but he looked straight at me. So, speaking directly to him, I stopped six paces away and said, "If you're there when I get there, I'm going to cut off your leg. And then we're going to fight."

They broke just before I reached them.

The story has a sad ending. Completely discredited, the gang broke up. Except for the four leaders that is. They stuck together and became a professional rock-and-roll group. Too bad—I never meant to start anything like that.

The power of the truth never ceases to amaze me. Sometime after I had moved to Chicago, I was in Kansas City on a visit to speak at a banquet in behalf of the Ozanam Boys' Home. While I was there, my good friend Walt Bodine asked me to appear on his show, a two-hour radio program called *The Night Owl*, and I promised him I'd be over after the speech. The banquet took more time than I had expected, and it made me late for the show. Joe Wallace had promised to drive me to the studio, and Bill Larson came along for the ride. On the way to the studio, I switched on the car radio when we were a couple of blocks from the station, and was just in time to hear Bodine come on the air. I was astonished to hear him say: "This is Walt Bodine with *The Night Owl* show, and tonight we have as our special guest Mr. Bill Sands, who will talk about the now famous Kansas City Rat Pack." This announcement was followed by a break for the commercial. I turned to Joe Wallace and said, "What the hell is the Rat Pack?"

Joe had less than two minutes to fill me in.

"The Rat Pack is a gang of Kansas City delinquents," he said. "Most of them come from Johnson County, and they're from good homes too. They've been accused of everything from smoking marijuana and holding sex orgies to malicious destruction and strong-arm robbery. Reach into my brief case and you'll find a bunch of articles about them. They're headline news."

I pulled out the articles and glanced through them quickly. The Rat Pack was indeed headline news. And I knew what Joe meant when he said they were from good homes. Johnson County has the second-highest per-capita income in the country, and its school system is acknowledged to be the finest there is.

The commercial break was just ending when we reached the radio station, so we switched off the car radio and ran for the studio. As I walked into the broadcast room, I saw that Walt Bodine was not alone. There were three hard-looking youngsters clustered around a microphone, their faces hostile and sullen.

"Ladies and gentlemen," Walt said when he saw me, "Bill Sands has just walked into our studio, and I am about to introduce him to three members of our infamous Kansas City Rat Pack and ask him to attempt to reform them here tonight with all of you listening."

I said nothing. What could I say?

He beckoned me to the table while he was saying, "Bill, what would you like to tell these three boys?"

"Well, the first thing I'd like to say is that I understand the Rat Pack is a gang of pretty tough kids. Right?"

"Right," Walt said. The boys said nothing.

"Are you guys really members of the Rat Pack?" I asked them.

I saw immediately that if I depended on them for help and conversation, I was going to be out of luck. They just looked at me defiantly, and they didn't utter a sound.

"Well," I went on, "I know a little bit about you and why you're here. I wonder how much you guys know about me?"

They looked at each other. Then one boy muttered, "Nothing."

"Okay," I said. "I'll tell you a little about myself." In doing so, I bore down heavily on the prison portion of my life—I even showed them the mashed nose and the crooked once-broken fingers. They continued to glare, but I knew I had caught their interest.

"I have an idea," I said finally. "You guys are running in a pack, and as far as I can see you are a pack of three. Well, it just happens that two guys brought me here, so I'll tell you a little bit about my two friends. One of them is Joe Wallace, and the other is Bill Larson."

Neither Joe nor Bill spoke at all during the broadcast, but they had come into the broadcast room with me. I told the boys briefly the stories of these two men, who had, between them, served almost thirty years in prison.

"You guys are supposed to be fairly tough," I said. "How would the three of you like to take on the three of us?" I stopped and waited.

The silence to the radio audience must have seemed interminable. In the studio, the three boys looked at each other, and then at Joe and Bill and me. None of them spoke, but their expressions eloquently said, Hey, that's not fair, you're taking advantage of us.

"Anyway," I continued, "we've been where you're headed. Believe me that among the three of us we can tell you about it."

It was time for another commercial break. And during the commercial I had the opportunity for the first time to say something privately to the kids.

"I'm sorry," I said, "I don't like this any better than you do. Walt is a good friend of mine, and I hope we give him a good show. But I don't want to put you down in front of your friends who might be listening. If you don't like what I'm saying when we're on the air, then interrupt and tell me so. Otherwise your friends will think you're chicken." The boys seemed impressed. I thought they were softening a little.

When the engineer in the glass-control booth gave the signal that we were back on the air, I said, "Tell me something. Are you guys totally happy with the life you're leading? Does everybody like you? Do you like them? Is everything smooth and easy? Or are there troubles?"

Not one of the boys would answer.

"I would assume you have some troubles. Am I right?"

"Yeah." The mutter seemed to come from the three of them.

"Am I also right that you're sick and tired of listening to adults who tell you to be sober and virtuous while they themselves are getting drunk and cheating on their husbands and wives? Am I right in assuming that you are tired of listening to adults who tell you to obey the law and then charge right ahead and cheat Uncle Sam out of every dollar they can get away with on their income taxes? Am I right in assuming that you have found better friends and more loyal friends in your Rat Pack than you can in church and in your home? Am I right in assuming that you have completely rebelled against the miserable and hypocritical world in which we live?"

The faces were beginning to break, and the nods of assent were noticeably warmer.

"Well," I said, "as you can gather, I think just the way you do. I don't like hypocrites or weaklings any better than you do. But I've found a way to stay strong and at the same time maintain both my happiness and my freedom. And I've done it the hard way. So has Joe and so has Bill. I've done time in a solitary cell, and yet I'm here tonight in Kansas City as the honored speaker at a banquet a lot of good people are holding for a worthy cause.

"Wouldn't you rather be doing that when you're grown men than doing time in solitary? Would you like me to teach you the things I know? Or are you so damn dumb that you have to learn them—if you ever manage to learn them—the way I did? If I tell you I know a way you can still be solid and tough and maintain your own code and in so doing achieve happiness, would you be willing to listen to it?"

The reserve was gone.

"Yeah, man," one said. And the others nodded.

"Okay," I said. "You've got to start with the first step, which is to face the truth about yourself and the world around you. That may sound easy, but it's not. I can't get you to do it in one short radio show, but I'll tell you what I will do. If you're game, I'll arrange for Joe Wallace to act as your friend and your guide. He'll take you into the prison with him, and he'll show it to you like it really is. He'll teach you what he knows to be true. Would you be willing to take that kind of counseling?"

At the end of the two-hour show the boys had agreed to be counseled by Joe Wallace. Moreover they had admitted on the air that they had *always* wanted and needed the kind of help and counseling that we were offering them. Before the show had ended, three more members of the Rat Pack who had been listening on their radios showed up at the studio because they too wanted and needed help.

I will probably never forget the last words that were said on that show.

"We've been talking together for almost two hours," I said. "And we're not finding it such a hard thing to do. Yet I see in the papers that your probation officer says he can't get through to you. Obviously, neither can your parents. I'm an adult, and now the four of us are friends. What's so different about me?"

One boy answered, "Man, you listen."

"What do you mean, I listen?" I said. "I've been doing well over half the talking for the last two hours."

"Not with your ears, man, but you listen."

After the radio show Joe Wallace did indeed successfully counsel the boys we had met that night. They left the Rat Pack and went back to school. They've been doing all right ever since.

Sometime later, when we had opened prerelease classes in several prisons, including Chino in southern California, I got a phone call from a Kentucky school-teacher. He was a man I didn't know, and he asked in great consternation if I would talk to his son Larry, who was in trouble. Larry had been arrested several times for burglary, but so far he had served only short jail sentences. Each time he had been released in the custody of his father. As a schoolteacher and a former Marine Corps officer, his father enjoyed a degree of status in his town, but unfortunately Larry didn't share the community's attitude at all. He considered school-teaching a sucker's game, and he had nothing but contempt for his father. He had dropped out of school himself, and he made heroes of the toughest and most lawless men he could find—among them several ex-convicts.

The beef that prompted the father to call me was another burglary—no different from the preceding ones. The judge who had heard the case had decided that if Larry remained unrepentant, he would have to serve a stretch in reform school. At the same time the judge—who had read *My Shadow* and shared my view that reform schools are often schools in crimi-

nal technique—was reluctant to send any youngster, and especially the son of a respectable and conscientious father, to such
a place without making one more effort. So he offered to suspend the sentence on one condition—that the father arrange
for him to talk with me.

I was in California when I received the phone call. My
response was to tell Larry's father frankly that I thought a
conversation with me would do the boy no good at all.

"What you're suggesting," I told him, "is that I solve in
a half-hour or so a problem that it's taken years to create. It
would be a miracle if any good came of it."

The father emphasized that the boy either talked to me or
he would have to enter reform school immediately. So I said,
"All right, send him on out. I'll do what I can."

Larry had an uncle living in California, and the uncle met
him at the plane and brought him to Chino, where the new
prerelease class was meeting that same night. I met them at
the gate only five minutes before the class began, and simply
suggested to the boy that he come along with me.

It was an exceptionally good class that night, and when I
was called upon to speak at the end, I could see that the boy
was impressed, though he was trying hard not to show it.

There were just thirty minutes left when I took the podium,
and I began by saying, "I normally comment on what you men
have been talking about, but tonight I'm going to point a finger
at someone you haven't met before. You will have noticed that
we have a very young man at our meeting tonight among the
visitors. His name is Larry Darin—and this is his story."

I told the men how Larry happened to be there. Then I
asked each of the members of our committee to join me at
the podium and to stand in a line facing the boy. Larry's face,
when I pointed to him directly, reflected a combination of

embarrassment and apprehension over what might be coming. It also showed defiance. He had been talked to before.

"Larry," I began, "these seven men are my very good friends. They are nice guys, good heads, and they are also solid cons. They can tell you far better than I what kind of life you're buying for yourself. I'd like you to meet them."

The man nearest me was a man I'll call Breezy. He is built a little like an Olympic weightlifting champion. I said to him, "Breezy, tell this boy what you're in for and what you think of him."

"Larry," Breezy said, "I'm a two-time loser. My last beef was a robbery-murder. You think it's cute to be tough, boy? Well, I'm tough—so tough I broke a man's neck by accident while I was trying to rob him. That was twenty-two years ago, and I've spent every day of those twenty-two years in some joint or other."

Breezy smashed one hand into the other and then went on, "I don't like it in these joints, kid, and neither would you. I know what I'm talking about. I've got twenty-two years of experience. And the toughest thing I've ever done is to face the truth about myself and then try to change."

The next man, whom I shall call Richie, is tall and slender—he looks for all the world like a professional man about six years out of college. When it was his turn to speak, he said, "My name is Richie Seiler. Maybe you think because your father is a schoolteacher you're different. That you'll never be just another number in a joint. Well, my father was something too. And I was given a good education. This is my third stretch, and I'm in as a habitual criminal. I don't know if I'll ever get out. I committed a lot of stupid little crimes, and I've done time in a lot of stupid joints. I don't like it. You wouldn't like it either. Change, kid."

As one man after another spoke, it was obviously beginning to dawn on Larry that prison was not the place he wanted to be in. But he held his face stiff and defiant, until the last speaker began.

This was a man named Bill Burns, our coordinator. He looks the way Sugar Ray Robinson looked before he had twenty too many fights.

"Kid," Bill said, "these guys are all telling you to stay out of joints, and I guess you think we're all pretty eager to see you reform. Well, maybe the others are, but I'm not. I don't care. If you want to look up to guys like me and these other cons, then you're the biggest sucker the world has ever seen and I don't give a damn what happens to you. If you want to spend your life in a joint, come right on in. You'll be welcome by a lot of guys I know. But maybe you won't think it's so great when some big dude starts to kiss you on the neck and tell you what you're going to do for him. The scum of the earth lives in these prisons, kid. If that's what you want to be, come join us."

When we left the prison I bought Larry a hamburger and spent a half-hour with him. He was quiet at first. But then he remarked, "Those guys are pretty tough, aren't they?"

"Yeah," I said. "Tough enough."

He paused thoughtfully. Then he went on, "I bet an ex-marine could take them on though. What do you think?"

"Maybe so," I said.

Another thoughtful pause.

And then—"You know, a schoolteacher isn't a bad thing to be, is it?"

When he'd finished his hamburger Larry rejoined his uncle. I never saw him again.

I did hear of him again though. More than a year later, I got a letter from his father. Larry had gone back to school and was doing well, his father wrote, and he wasn't causing any more trouble.

"He's still a pretty tough kid," his father wrote, "but he has it under control now."

Every Seventh Step prerelease class puts out a weekly bulletin. The Chino group wrote up the experience with Larry. When the Lansing committee read of this, they decided to try to get local delinquents to visit the Lansing class.

One of the squarejohns who regularly attended the Lansing class had a nephew named Hank Brown who had dropped out of high school, served several jail sentences, and was a general all-round troublemaker. When the committee began to talk about having youngsters visit the class, the squarejohn immediately thought of Hank. The next week he brought him along to the meeting. Hank only watched the class. But the next week he brought along his father, also Hank Brown, who was a professional photographer in Kansas City. The Lansing committee talked to Hank Junior much as the Chino committee had talked to Larry, and when the boy and his father left Lansing that night, they had the first friendly conversation they had had in years.

Both father and son continued to attend. The convicts never addressed any of their remarks to the father, but after weeks of watching them work on his son, he got up in class one night.

"You all talk about facing the truth about yourselves in this class," he said. "Well, I have a truth I think I ought to face. My son has been in and out of trouble for years, and people say he's a rotten kid. I want to tell you I've been a rotten father. I drink more than I ought to, and I don't give the boy the kind of attention he needs. That's the truth. I intend to change."

He was as good as his words. Within weeks the youngster had straightened out completely. He had dropped out of high school, but now he took equivalency examinations, passed them, and entered college. The boy is now doing magnificently there, and his father has stopped drinking and begun to devote his free time to his family. The first time I met his wife she told me our committee had not only saved her son but had also restored her husband to her.

A good thing gets around. Deputy sheriffs from Kansas started bringing their problem kids directly from their jails into the class at Lansing. The success of this experiment was so phenomenal that the number of boys who were being brought into Lansing by jailers or probation officers or judges soon made it necessary for our juvenile program to be formalized. There is now a Seventh Step hour just for juveniles after every class. It is run by the prerelease class committees, and it is one of the most heartening aspects of our work. While the boys are inside the prison, the committee has a chance to strip the glamor from being bad and attach a little glamor to being good. It makes an impression.

Every Seventh Step chapter is required by our national bylaws to work with juveniles. We have had escapees from reform school turn themselves in to us in San Francisco. A boy turned in his gun in San Jose. And Bill Larson in Topeka has so many cases to his credit that he has had to set aside a separate file cabinet just to keep track of them.

Chapter 16

I t looked like a police convention, or a combined police convention and dog show. The Kansas City police has a K-9 Corps, and it looked as though every officer in town was there with his dog.

Our destination had been the La Salle Bar, but now we turned off into a nice dark sidestreet and parked. The La Salle Bar was the known hangout of every hot crook in town and we were all ex-convicts—and one of us was on parole.

Wrestler said he'd get out and go to the bar on foot, adding, "There's no use you going, Bill. You're out of touch. The guys wouldn't talk to you. But me, I know everybody in town who's on the take."

Off he went, his frame huge under the street lights, his shadow even larger.

Here was I—a respectable citizen of Chicago, a speaker who was making frequent appearances on national television, the author of a best-selling book—dodging the Kansas City police at four o'clock in the morning, I was sweating so hard that I was sure the police dogs would smell it. My companions and I were not exactly breaking the law—but we were certainly skirting it. We were looking for an ex-convict with a police bullet in his back. And we were planning—if we found him—to give him any help we could.

How had we got into this mess? Easily. Joe Wallace and I had flown in to attend a perfectly normal Seventh Step club meeting only a few hours before. When a call came in, Joe answered the phone. What put me on the alert was the tension I heard in his voice as he told the caller, "Hold it till I can get on another line."

I saw that he looked strained and troubled as he hurried into a private office and closed the door, so I went over and hung up the clubroom instrument. No one else seemed to notice how upset he was. He was in the office for several minutes, then opened the door and gestured to me. I went in and shut the door behind me.

"Big trouble, Bill. That was Bob Hacker. You don't know him, he's not one of ours. He's got Jim Crane up in his room."

"Jim Crane?"

"He *is* one of ours," Joe explained. "Tall, good-looking young guy. Just got out of Lansing a couple of weeks ago. Friend of Ezra's."

I remembered, then, but vaguely. "What's the beef, Joe?"

"Jim's got a thirty-eight slug just above the kidney. Bob Hacker thinks he's about to die on him."

"Police?"

"Yes, but Bob didn't know much more than that. Jim walked several miles to get to him, and passed out almost at once after he got there. He's lost a lot of blood, and the wound's beginning to swell badly. Bob's tried a couple of doctors that he's got connections with, but they're not around just now."

"What did you tell him?"

"To get him to a hospital as fast as possible, no matter how, and to knock him out with a rock if he wouldn't go. That the most important thing was to save his life."

"For Christ's sake, Joe, I hope he didn't take you literally." Jim surely wouldn't go voluntarily and if Bob hit him, the blow would probably kill him. "Where are they?"

"In Bob's apartment."

"Where's that?"

"I don't know," Joe admitted.

"Well, find out!"

"What are we going to do?"

"We're going to find Crane first, and then decide," I told him.

As Joe started out to the door, I called him. "Wait a minute, Joe. How many of the guys in the club can we really depend upon in a deal like this?"

Joe thought for a moment.

"I'm sure we can depend on Wrestler and Charley Moore. You know the rest better than I do."

Walking into the clubroom, I singled out Moore and Wrestler, and asked them to wait there. Then I asked Jim Rayburn and Spud Barrett to take Pony back to the motel. After that I looked over at the other men, all of whom were wearing expressions of curiosity.

"The rest of you clear out. We have a problem to tackle you don't want to know about."

I filled in Wrestler and Charley as to what was up, telling them we had to find out where Bob Hacker lived.

"He's on the take. Nobody's going to know where he lives," Wrestler contributed. "Not unless we can find somebody he's working with."

Charley spoke up.

"How about the La Salle Bar? Everybody on the take hangs out there. Somebody's sure to be there who knows. And if the guys won't talk to somebody who's been out of circulation as long as you and I have, Bill, they'll talk to Wrestler."

So we took off. And this is how we came to run into the police convention. We couldn't be sure that the police department was there on the same errand as ourselves, but it didn't seem like the best place in the world for a carful of ex-convicts.

Wrestler wasn't gone nearly as long as the time seemed to us. When he came back, he muttered an address to Joe and started folding his frame into the car.

"Not Bob's place," he said. "But the guy who lives there has been pranking with him. These cops *are* looking for him."

Joe drove off slowly, anxious to avoid attracting police notice. Suddenly he asked, "Bill, do you remember Jack Trellyon, a few years ago?"

"A few years ago? I saw him a few *weeks* ago."

Charley cut in with a question. "Was he limping?"

Slightly puzzled, I answered, "No, not at all. Why?"

Joe waited, as though expecting someone else to speak. Then he said, "Four years ago he took a slug that broke his leg. I heard the guy who fixed him up wasn't a doc, and never had been."

Silently we drove along. There was not much civilian traffic on the street. Every other car we saw had a police shield on the side, and the ones without it were probably detective cruisers. Foot cops leading—or being led by—K-9 dogs were trying store doors and going in and out of apartments and tenements and rooming houses.

Then Charley burst out. "Oh hell! I was the doc who fixed up Jack. Took out the slug and set the leg, and last time I saw him he said it didn't even hurt when it was raining. I can fix up Crane—if we find him."

He went on to name the prison where he had been a pharmacist, and the other where he had worked in the infirmary as a surgical assistant.

We asked him what he needed in the way of instruments. He said he could get everything he didn't have at home at an all-night drugstore.

"All I really need is a place to work in."

"Get your stuff together and take it around to my motel room," I told him. Somebody whispered "fall guy" to me. I think it was myself. But it seemed to me that my room was the last place in town where the police would look.

We dropped Charley off where he could get a cab. The cop cars had thinned out. They must have had a tip that Jim Crane was holed-up near the La Salle Bar. If he wasn't, some stool pigeon was going to lose his place in the breadline. Nobody in this car was going to bruise his hands wringing them over that.

By the time we reached the address Wrestler had picked up in the La Salle, police activity was down to zero. Several miles from the bar Wrestler pointed to a house, telling Joe to stop there. Then he went up to the door and knocked, for he knew the man who lived there, at least by sight.

Cautiously, but at once, the door was opened. The man who came out looked over Wrestler, then nodded. We could hear him asking who was waiting in the car. Wrestler said, "Bill Sands and Joe Wallace."

"Let's see."

We climbed out. When we could be clearly seen in the light from the streetlamp, the man nodded, moving his head as if he had a glass neck.

"Okay. What do you want?"

"Bob Hacker," said Wrestler. "He called Joe Wallace before, but they broke off before he could give his address."

The man—whose name I never learned—moved his jaw sideways, as though he wanted to chew that up before he bit off any more information. Finally he swallowed.

"What's it all about?"

"You don't want to know," Wrestler shook his head. "Hell, man, don't be so chinchy. We're all solid guys, and you know it."

The guy raised his chin again.

"I guess it's okay. Bob lives across the street where you can see the lights."

Then the door closed. But, after all, two hours before dawn you don't have that many lighted windows to choose from.

Nothing in my life—and I guess nothing in Wrestler's or Joe's—had taught us how to walk up on a wounded and possibly delirious man with a gun. We lined up in the street, then I tilted up my head and bawled up toward the lighted window. "Jim, it's Bill Sands, Joe Wallace, and Wrestler."

And I don't think the other two minded my giving myself top billing.

No answer. We moved closer and once again I tried. My voice projects, as they say in show business, but the audience that night wasn't responsive. After I had yelled two or three times, we went into the downstairs hall, through an unlocked door.

Telling the other two to stay downstairs in case the people in the lower flat—if any—had heard my one-man serenade, I hurried upstairs. Then, squeezed against the wall next to the door, I put out my fist and knocked, saying, "It's Bill Sands, it's Bill Sands."

I don't remember how often I repeated this, but I had no more answer than I had had in the street. So I tried the door, but it was locked. At last I went downstairs again and out onto the porch. I needed fresh air. But the moment I was on the porch, alone, a man came out of the shadows. He was holding a .45—it looked like a .90, if there is a gun that big—on my belly.

"Got a name?"

Considering that I had been yelling it all over the neighborhood for quite a while, repetition seemed unnecessary. But he had the gun. I spoke up.

"Who's with you?"

Raising my voice so that the two men inside could hear me, I said, "Wrestler and Joe Wallace."

Right on cue, they came out into the light from the porch lamp, and the man asked, "Wrestler, is this really Bill Sands?"

"Yes."

The .45 went into the waistband of the stranger's belt. Putting out his hand, he said, "I'm Bob Hacker. I'm glad you guys are here. I got Jim in a closed-up bar not too far away. We got to have some medical help for him."

"We've got it, and a car," I told him. "Let's go."

In the car, I sat next to Bob Hacker, who began, "I've heard about you, Bill. I'm still on the take, and you've gone square, but they tell me you're still solid clear through. Who you got lined up for Jim?"

"Charley Moore."

He swore.

"Christ, I should have thought of him." Then, leaning forward, he said, "Right over there, Joe."

"There" was a small, detached building which had been a bar so long ago that I barely remembered some of the brands advertised by the dingy signs. It was a good hideout—no cop was likely to investigate it. We didn't go in with Hacker to get Crane. Through any kind of semi-delirious haze, Crane was most likely to recognize Hacker—and we weren't forgetting that the wounded man still had his gun. When Bob reappeared, half-carrying and half-dragging Crane, I remembered Jim from Lansing.

I remembered him, but he certainly had changed. In the joint he had been a good-looking kid, carrying his six feet three inches with a good deal of grace. Now he was drenched with sweat and covered with filth, and as limp as the bar-rag in a ten-cent wino joint.

We were all out of the car except Joe. We pushed Jim into the front seat and I got in on the right side to hold him up and shield him from passing cars as much as possible. There wouldn't have been room for Wrestler up front, and I was the second-biggest shield. The other men got in the back and we started off. Across Crane's slumped body Joe asked, "Sure you want us to use your motel room?"

"Charley's already headed there," I reminded him. Then, turning in my seat as best I could, I spoke to the men behind. I thought Jim wouldn't hear me. He felt as if he'd passed out.

"We've got to cover ourselves in case we're stopped. All five of us have records, and Jim is trying to run with a cop slug in his back. If we get the siren and the red light, leave me to do the talking. But they might separate us to check my story, so here it is. Crane went to Hacker, Hacker called us because Jim was afraid that if he tried to turn himself in, the first cop who saw him might shoot first and ask questions later. We're taking him to the motel so that he can call his parole officer and get picked up in a state car. We'd figured that was the only way Crane could get medical help without the risk of getting shot some more."

The Wrestler and Joe muttered their okays, but Bob Hacker was silent. And I had been wrong when I thought Jim was too far gone to hear me. There was even a little strength in his voice as he asked, "Are you really turning me in?"

"Not unless that's what you want," I said. "But if we're stopped, there's no use your getting four other guys busted too."

Bob Hacker spoke up. "Bill's right, Jim."

All Jim Crane said was, "I'm sure glad you guys came."

Not another word did he say on the way to the motel, but I could hear his teeth grating so hard that I seemed to feel it all through my arms. And he was reeking of sweat.

In the motel room we found my wife, Pony, with another couple. Luckily the man was an ex-con like the rest of us. And, thank God, Charley was there. He didn't have all the surgical equipment to be found in a hospital, but he had enough. We put Jim down on one of the beds, I helped him get down a double shot of whiskey, and he started talking.

He had broken parole all right. He had made a U-turn! A policeman, stopping to let a K-9 dog out of his car, saw him and gave chase. But it wasn't Jim's car—it had been lent him by a girl who had a husband. So Jim stepped on the gas and tried to outrun the cruiser. The cop radioed for help. Somebody got the slug into the car and into Jim's back. The slug had been slowed down by cutting through parts of the auto, otherwise it would certainly have come out through his chest and killed him.

Not that he was in good shape anyway. After jockeying into a throughway he had sideswiped another car, knocking it into a ditch, and had kept on going. If the girlfriend's husband ever got his car back, he would have quite a repair bill. At present it was still ditched some eighteen miles away—Jim had *walked* the eighteen miles back to Hacker's place.

Charley was still staring into the wound with the help of a little flashlight. One of the men who had not gone with us came in from the other room, and said, "Charley, if you touch that wound, you're violating your parole."

None of us had seen my wife come in too, but we certainly heard her now. She said firmly, "Only if somebody in this room talks."

Pony and I had our troubles later, but I'm proud of the way she acted in that motel room.

Charley grunted that he was ready to probe if that was still what Jim Crane wanted. He helped me get Jim into position to swallow more whiskey. Then I started talking.

"Jim, you were in the program out at the joint. You know the pitch—a man who gets out of prison is sure to go back in if he doesn't stop kidding himself that he can get away with breaking the law. But it's your business. Nobody can change someone else. So if you want, Charley will take out the bullet and I'll give you fifty bucks, and none of us saw you tonight."

"Or what?" asked Jim. The whiskey had put some color back into his chalky face.

"So far all you've done is make a U-turn and run from a cop. If you tell me to, I'll call your parole officer, Harrity. He'll get you into a hospital and he'll see to it that some cop doesn't blast first and ask afterward. You'll have a real doctor in a real operating room, and you can quit being a professional thief on the run. Harrity won't be too rough—he's pretty square."

Jim half-closed his eyes. I knew what he was thinking. Every con in the Seventh Step has thought the same thing.

When you stop lying to yourself, you know that every crook gets caught sooner or later, and you decide that you are tired of doing time.

At last he said, "There's the car I sideswiped. If the driver's dead, I've had it."

"He'll be just as dead when they catch up with you."

He winced. But he never asked me if I would turn him in without his own consent. He knew none of us would.

Finally he said, "Call Harrity." He swallowed, and beat with his clenched fist on the bed. "I'm scared, but call Harrity. Be sure and tell him it was my own idea."

Bob Hacker nodded. "You're doing the only thing, Jim. Otherwise they'd nail you in forever."

And he went into the other room to phone. He changed his voice while he talked to Harrity. Then he and the other two guys on parole—Wrestler and Charley—left us.

The man who had warned Charley about breaking parole if he helped Jim Crane was fairly high in Seventh Step. He proceeded to read the constitution and all its amendments to me. He was sore at Joe Wallace for getting me into this.

"You've got too much to lose these days," he told me. "Joe and Wrestler and Charley should have kept you out of it."

"What you are trying to tell me," I retorted, "is that it was okay for me when nobody knew me, to be solid and to work for these guys. But that now that I'm known, you want me to turn my back when the chips go down. Sure I've got a lot to lose. I've got the whole Seventh Step to lose. And I'll lose it— we shall all lose everything we have put into it—if I don't go with the first team any time and every time we get a call like the one we got tonight."

Finally I convinced him, and now he is one of the most useful men in the movement.

Crane got out of that evening well. Harrity helped him into a hospital and went to bat for him with the officer who had chased him. And the officer admitted that Crane had only acted scared, not belligerent. The man who had been sideswiped had not been hurt, and on learning that Crane might do a long stretch for breaking parole, he refused to press charges. So Crane received a thirty-day suspended sentence. No sweat to that.

Which makes it a story with a happy ending—except for one thing.

A few weeks later Jim Crane tried to jimmy coin boxes in a laundromat and was caught.

This makes it a story with an unhappy ending but for another thing. A few weeks after Crane stepped back into the web, Bob Hacker showed up at the Seventh Step Club, announcing that he was going straight.

"Since when?" I asked. "Tomorrow?"

"Believe it or not, I haven't pulled a job since that night we all churned around on the Crane deal. That night you guys on the square showed up a lot better than a taker like me."

So far, Bob Hacker has stuck to his resolve. So have a lot of other men. For every one Jim Crane there have been nine or ten Bob Hackers.

And we haven't given up on Jim Crane. Perhaps next time, with the help of the Seventh Step, he'll make it.

Chapter 17

I suppose any effort that attracts widespread attention also attracts widespread opposition. Why I don't know. It seems to be a fact of life.

My first encounter with this fact came as a surprise. I had accepted three invitations, spaced fairly close together, to lecture in Minnesota. The first one went off well. It was at a fund-raising dinner for Brother de Paul's Roncalli House on an island between the Twin Cities, a hostel that feeds thousands of indigents and cares for the needs of newly released prisoners.

The second engagement looked highly promising. Warden Jack G. Young invited me to address the prison population at his Minnesota State Reformatory in St. Cloud. The appearance of the institution startled me, for it looked much more like a maximum-security prison than like a reformatory. But Warden Young seemed all right. He told me he was a "progressive penologist," and he agreed to have his staff—as well as the inmates—attend the talk. So I gave the same sort of speech I usually give in a prison, receiving rocking applause from the prisoners. There was no response from the prison staff members, but I thought nothing of that. Usually I don't hear much applause from guards.

But then, a few weeks later, I gave two talks at the little town of Austin, Minnesota—a speech to the high-school students in the afternoon and one to adults in the evening. To my flattered surprise, the mayor, the chief of police, and several other town officials were at the earlier gathering. Since they would hear me again in the nighttime open meeting, they seemed gluttons for Sands. Both the afternoon speech and the night session went off well—good applause, interested, intelligent questions, and even a key to the city from the mayor.

But when he could talk to me in private, the program chairman who had invited me to Austin showed me a memo he had received—a photostat that apparently had been circulated in every town in Minnesota and probably elsewhere. It was from Warden Young at St. Cloud, and said, in part:

Those of us who are exposed daily to clinical problems rather jointly agree that Mr. Sands was an excellent textbook example of a psychopath . . . and I am taking steps to alert other correctional institutions so that they will not fall into the same trap as I did.

I didn't know then, I still don't know, what I had done or said that frightened Warden Young so much. But when I was invited to speak at the Texas State Prison—Huntsville—I thought of changing my whole approach. Dr. George Beto, director of the Texas Board of Corrections, admitted that he shared some of my apprehension. For all I know he may have received one of Warden Young's photo-stated memos. But Dr. Beto knew both Clinton Duffy and Tennessee Ernie Ford, both of whom, he said, had spoken highly of me. So I went ahead and gave almost the same speech I had used at St. Cloud.

I wasn't left in doubt for very long. While the prisoners were still applauding Dr. Beto came forward, took the microphone and said, "I was hesitant about having Mr. Sands here today because I had heard some very bad reports of him. But his talk has been one of the most beneficial ever heard in this prison." Then, turning to me, he concluded, "Bill Sands, I'm glad to welcome you to Huntsville, and I invite you back to the Texas prison system any time you can come."

But Warden Young wasn't the only one to see the danger in our program. Some time before, I had had a brief correspondence with a man named Pete Pearson, of the Canadian Broadcasting Corporation. He wrote that he would like me to talk on his network—but he wanted me to talk only about my experiences with Caryl Chessman. I declined. I don't like to talk or broadcast about Chess because other people know much more about him than I do. Pony, in particular, knew him well years after I last saw him. So I suggested that I talk about the Seventh Step program instead, but Pearson replied that we weren't needed in Canada because the prison system there was so far ahead of the United States that reform was unnecessary.

I wrote in reply suggesting that he drop in on some prison when he wasn't expected, and, using his influence as a government employee, look around on his own rather than taking the escorted tour. He did more than that. He went into the old St. Vincent de Paul prison, taking with him a camera and soundcrew who were able to photograph the appalling inside of this rat-infested womb of misery. Pete later showed the film on the controversial CBC show (since canceled) *This Hour Has Seven Days*. The resulting public outcry ended only when the government was forced to announce that the St. Vincent de Paul prison would be torn down. Pete had let it be known that his visit to the prison had resulted from my letter. Now, he wanted me to broadcast in Canada again—and this time he placed no restrictions on the subject matter.

I flew from Chicago to Toronto. There, as I was going through the immigration station, I was jerked out of line by one of the inspecting officers, who asked if he hadn't seen me on the *Johnny Carson Show* recently.

That made me smile broadly. What lecturer or performer doesn't like to meet a fan? When the officer—customs, as I remember his badge—said that I had put on "a rather remarkable performance," I thanked him. But it wasn't meant as a compliment. He asked me—and now I could smell the bullying policeman—if I was not engaged in opposing capital punishment and exposing prison brutality.

Certainly I was not going to deny this charge. And since he had seen me on TV the question was foolish. So I nodded. He waved me to a chair and handed me a form to fill out.

"Just routine," he said. "All entertainers entering Canada have to answer these questions."

"I'm not here as an entertainer," I said. "I have been invited in by CBC as an author and lecturer."

He nodded as though that made all the difference in the world. In a minute I found out that it didn't, for he said, "In that case, I'll just have to ask you a few questions. Now, first, have you ever been in prison?"

Time was against me. A news conference had been set up at a hotel in town, and I would be late for it.

"I thought you said you saw me on Johnny Carson's show? You know I'm an ex-convict."

"Then you admit that you're trying to enter Canada illegally?" He sounded only mildly triumphant.

"Of course not," I retorted. "I'm here in answer to a request from a government agency—the Canadian Broadcasting Corporation."

"Mr. Sands, it is against Canadian law for an ex-convict to immigrate."

"Immigrate? I'm coming in today, broadcasting tonight, leaving in the morning. Is that your idea of immigration?"

He shrugged.

"Sorry. I'm just here to see that the immigration laws are obeyed."

Obviously this was not his idea. Someone far above him had stationed him there to stop me. And he stopped me dead. He wouldn't even let me go to a phone to call Pete Pearson.

Fortunately I did not have to phone. When I didn't show up at the hotel news conference, the program director called the airport and found out that I was there and the plight I was in. At once CBC sent a mobile TV crew to the field to film the story, with the reporters from the hotel following in its wake.

The officer who stopped me may have been more important than his uniform indicated. When he heard about the mobile crew on its way out to interview me, he had an Air Canada plane bound for Cleveland stopped on the runway. I was put on board, and the crew was given orders not to let me off again in Canada.

On the way from Canada the entire crew came back one by one to apologize for the officer's behavior, and to ask me not to judge their country by the narrow-mindedness of a few officials. Even had I been foolish enough to do so, my opinion would have changed again pretty quickly. For an hour after I reached Chicago Pete Pearson phoned from Toronto with apologies and a suggestion.

As he explained it, since CBC was a government agency, I had been "invited by the host and turned away by the butler." His proposal was that I should return to Canada, this time through Buffalo. He wanted me to go there on foot—across the Friendship Bridge to Fort Erie, Ontario—with CBC arranging for TV cameras and newsmen to cover the march.

I was not allowed to enter. But we had made our point. Pearson had a lovely story to run on television, and overnight I became a headliner in the Canadian press. One paper pointed out that Canada had readily admitted George Lincoln Rockwell, head of the American Nazi party. Others demanded a Parliamentary investigation—and got it. The debate was protracted. When it was over, I received an informal apology from the government of Canada—I was sent a special pass allowing me to enter the country at any time I chose to appear on the government television network.

The next criticism directed against us was really a great favor, since it gave Clement Stone and me an idea that greatly helped Seventh Step. The critic was a reviewer for the stately *Monthly Journal of Penology*, a periodical certainly entitled to its opinion. In part, the review of *My Shadow Ran Fast* said:

Sands suggests the formation of prerelease classes for convicts conducted by ex-convicts rather than by correctional authorities . . . because the men inside prisons refuse, for the most part, to take moral lessons from the so-called do-gooders.

"I would make every sentence indeterminate, going from one year to life.

"I would install, in the place of men now on parole boards, M.D. psychiatrists, polygraph (lie detector) operators and men skilled in the use of sodium pentothal, hypnotism and every other technological advance that probes the human mind."

Such statements hardly present a philosophy of crime control which will impress people (such as Clinton Duffy, member of the California adult paroling authority, for example) who really understand crime and criminals.

Pony read the criticism first. Then she passed it on to me, and I read it over the phone to Clement Stone. He snorted gently, adding the mild comment, "You can't please every one."

"No," I said. "But I object strenuously to their citing Clinton Duffy as an authority *against* Seventh Step. He'd be the last person in the world to oppose what I'm trying to do."

"You're sure?"

"I'm absolutely certain that Seventh Step is in line with his entire philosophy. In fact, if he weren't so firmly retired, he would probably be out working for our foundation."

Clement Stone said, "He would?"

"Yes. In fact—"

"Call him up and ask him. He's just what we need."

While I waited for the long-distance call to go through, I began to have misgivings. Somehow or other, the idea of Clinton T. Duffy working for a bunch of ex-convicts wasn't right. And then I realized that it was the most right thing in the world. All through his career Warden Duffy had been working for convicts. If I put it that way . . .

The truth was, I couldn't sell this man. I could only drive him to the store and let him buy or not, as he wished. Nobody could pressure Clinton Duffy into doing anything, nobody could con him.

He recognized my voice as soon as I said, "Hi, warden, how's Mom?"

I came to the point at once.

"Warden, would you consider coming out of retirement and going to work again?"

"Well, I'm not looking for a job, Bill."

Warden Duffy knew about my Seventh Step work. The promotion tours had taken me to San Francisco several times, and each time I had visited the Duffys. So I skipped bringing him up to date, and made the proposition flat. Before Seventh Step could expand much farther—into new states, new institutions, new areas, such as juvenile delinquency—the program needed the advice and help of a professional penologist. And who could be better than Clinton Duffy?

Silence on the line. Then what I had expected—"I would have to give it some thought, of course." Of course. "Learn more of what you're doing. Only then could I really decide."

"Let me show you the program close up. Come to Kansas City, as a guest of the foundation, and go out to Lansing with me. Meet the class members and the squarejohns in the sponsorship group. I think you'll be impressed."

Another silence. But I could almost hear him thinking that a trip to the Middle West wouldn't commit him to anything.

"Okay, Bill. I'm free anytime next week."

At Kansas City there left the plane a stocky man with a strong, kindly face under a shock of white hair—Warden Duffy. I met him and drove him up to the Holiday Inn, where the marquee bore in large letters—KANSAS CITY WEL-COMES CLINTON DUFFY. The lobby of the motel was filled with newspapermen and television units ready to interview him. He chuckled softly.

"Bill, you're incorrigible."

We spent a busy weekend. Warden Duffy talked to Rue Holland and other squarejohns. He spent a long time at the clubroom, talking to the men on parole and release. His questions were so quiet that the men hardly realized that they were being cross-examined. Before it was time to visit the prison on Monday, Mr. Duffy knew as much about Seventh Step in Kansas as it was possible to know.

When we set out for Lansing on Monday, I was filled with pride. Bill Sands was going to walk into Kansas State Prison with Clinton T. Duffy at his side, as his friend. It seemed to me that grim Lansing was smiling in the sun.

Twenty-five years before, Clinton Duffy had taken over the world's largest prison on the heels of the bloodiest riot in the history of penology. The prison of which he became warden contained six thousand rioting, violent, hate-filled men. In the entire history of San Quentin no warden had ever walked into the Main Yard when the prisoners were there without a heavy guard. Had he done so, he would have been torn limb from limb, for to those six thousand men he was the man who denied them their freedom.

Like most prison Yards, the Main Yard at San Quentin is a vast area of concrete, surrounded on four sides by towering walls, patrolled by armed guards on raised catwalks. One day the steel door at the far end of this yard swung open and through it stepped a man in a blue suit. Behind him the door swung shut and was locked. The man was Clinton T. Duffy, the new warden, and he was alone with his prisoners. As casually as a housewife walks across her kitchen, he began walking across San Quentin's Main Yard.

There was a shocked silence. But it was followed by a sound never heard before in any prison, anywhere in the world. The sound of six thousand men cheering and applauding the man who kept them caged.

This was the beginning of Duffy's career as warden—ten minutes after his appointment as temporary warden. Until then he had been an obscure prison clerk. He remained as warden of San Quentin for twelve years, and throughout his tenure he walked through every part of the prison, at any time of the day or night, without an escort. Sometimes he walked with his wife on his arm. For twelve years he was welcome everywhere he appeared—even on Death Row, which housed men whom the law required him to execute.

The old miracle was repeated at Lansing. The prison population knew he was coming. Even as Warden Duffy was being formally greeted by the warden and his staff, I could hear unusual noises coming from inside the gates. A man singing as he walked along, another whistling—cheerful sounds to hear in that old, old monument to man's failure.

The warden had given Jim Post the honor of showing Warden Duffy around Lansing. As we went along, men who could not possibly have done time under Duffy at San Quentin—they were too young—would come up and grab his hand. Some of them said a few words, but many were too moved to talk.

What they saw in Clinton Duffy was integrity. He believed in humane and understanding treatment of men behind bars. He believed that men were sent to prison as punishment, not for punishment. But most of all, the men in prisons all over the country knew that Warden Duffy could be trusted. He had lived a long life without ever betraying anyone—convict, guard, or freeman.

There may be other men with the high standards and the complete honor of Clinton T. Duffy. There are certainly wardens who try to run their prisons with justice and humanity. But Warden Duffy has a special quality. Somehow he inspires convicts and guards alike to try harder.

I may sound like a kid who has found his idol. For all that I'm fortyish, balding, somewhat battered, that is just what I have done and continue to do. It is more than twenty-five years since Warden Duffy first visited the bitter, resentful kid I used to be in solitary. He has been my idol ever since.

Duffy talked at some length with each member of the inside committee headed by Ezra Kingsley and with many of the members of the class. Thereafter he spent two hours or more in conversation with Ezra himself. Obviously Duffy was impressed. He told me that the idea of a committee composed of men not eligible for parole, and therefore not influenced by selfish motives, was one of the most valuable things in the whole Seventh Step setup.

"What do you think of Ezra?" I asked.

"He would certainly be an asset to us on the outside. What is being done to get him out?"

"Rue Holland is leading a group of men—sponsors who know Ezra—to go before the board." I explained why Seventh Step had to stay away completely from this movement. "But there's no reason why I personally should not help."

"Do it, Bill," Duffy urged. "Do it! Ezra Kingsley has earned his chance for freedom."

The climax of the day was the class. I took a quick survey as we entered the larger classroom Ezra had obtained for the class. All the regulars were there. A few new faces had appeared—which was usual enough. In addition, a number of high officials in the state correctional system were in attendance—at last they had come to Lansing to sit in on a prerelease class. It was too bad that they had come to meet Warden Duffy rather than to learn about our program and what it was doing for the men and for the state of Kansas. But they were there at last. We had a very big opportunity.

Three hundred spirits hovered over that class—the spirits of the men already out and staying out under the Seventh Step program. Those unseen participants were the most important ones.

I watched Duffy closely as one convict after another took the podium and faced the inevitable barrage of questions from his peers. I could tell that he was fascinated and impressed by the way these men were helping each other to face the truth about themselves. Finally, when that part of the class ended, it was time for me to introduce Warden Duffy. I heard myself beginning with the old cliché—"the speaker needs no introduction"—and then words came to me.

So I said quietly that anyone who had read my book knew of my relationship to Warden Duffy and that anyone who hadn't, certainly knew his reputation. But, I said, there was one chapter I had never told.

"For about two years after leaving San Quentin I kept in touch with the warden and his wife. Then I stopped seeing them, stopped writing. I thought that just being out and staying free wasn't enough, that I ought to accomplish something substantial to show them, to prove that it had been worthwhile to give me back my life in San Quentin.

"Now I realize that it wasn't necessary. That the greatest gift I could give the Duffys, the great gift you men can give to the sponsors who help you out of prison, is simply to maintain your freedom and live constructively."

I turned to face Duffy, who was sitting to the left of the speaker's rostrum. His face was softened by compassion, just as it had been many years ago when I had cried out in my anguish "Nobody cares" and he had answered "I care."

Continuing the introduction, I said, "Warden Duffy, I have received all the credit for starting The Seventh Step Foundation and the program of prisoner remotivation. The credit is not mine—it is yours. Without you I would not be here. You literally gave me back my life when I was one of your prisoners. Everything I may do or accomplish I can trace directly to the love and the understanding you so abundantly gave.

"Perhaps I have found right here in this dreary prison the gift that I sought. My gift is the faces of these men and the hope behind those faces. Here are men trying, for the first time in their lives, to face the truths about themselves and the world around them, men who are trying and succeeding. The men in this room who are about to be released and the more than three hundred men who have preceded them are maintaining their freedom because of the truths that you taught me almost twenty-five years ago.

"My gift is the gift of truth. We have found a way to use truth to help men change. I would like here and now to dedicate this program and all of the lives it has changed to you, Warden Clinton T. Duffy."

I sat down.

Slowly Warden Duffy rose and walked to the rostrum. He faced, for him, a familiar scene—hundreds of upturned faces shining with hope, faith, and affection. The faces of our damned and our incarcerated. He was deeply moved.

"Before coming here to Kansas City, I went to Chicago to talk to Mr. W. Clement Stone. Then I passed two days in Kansas City talking to graduates of this class and to their sponsors and employers. I was impressed by the constructive attitudes of Seventh Step men. Here, tonight, I have seen the formation of those attitudes. Bill has asked me to join this movement and help it expand to other states, and I told him I would have to see your work before I let him know my decision. Now, I *have* seen your work, and I have formed this opinion. This may well be the greatest single advance that has ever been made in man's efforts to rehabilitate or remotivate men in prison."

The newsmen present were furiously taking notes, and as Duffy paused, I could hear the gentle whirr of the television news camera.

"Just before this meeting started," he continued, "one of the TV newsmen asked me how I would feel if I were to go to work for a man I had once confined in solitary. I did not have time to answer him, so I will answer now, I shall not be working *for* Bill Sands, but I will work *with* him. Together we will try to make a part of this world a better place to live in. How do I feel about that? I feel very proud to be working once again with my friend."

Chapter 18

The Kansas state board of paroles, who also act as the clemency board, agreed to a hearing for Ezra Kingsley. Rue Holland and I drove out to Topeka. I had just flown in from Chicago, and Rue filled me in on Ezra's chances.

"There are three possibilities," he said. "Clemency from the governor, of course. An appeal to a court to set aside his conviction as illegal. Or just a simple request to the pardons attorney to instruct the prison to correct the records, so that Ezra is given credit for already having served both sentences instead of one—usually sentences run concurrently."

I knew from my own experience about the concurrent thing. The judge had sentenced Ezra on two charges, but had failed to say whether the sentences were to succeed each other or to run concurrently. In the absence of a specific instruction, concurrence was held to be the rule.

I asked, "What do you mean about the illegal sentence?"

"The second one," Rue said. "The court didn't have juris-diction. That's how Carl Fry, Ezra's partner, got his sentence reversed. Ezra's should have been, too."

Of course. Fry had been Ezra's partner in crime. They had been tried in the same court, and what applied to one should apply to the other.

"We're a cinch, then," I said.

"If we take it easy and go very cautiously," Rue said. "If we ask the governor to reduce Ezra's time to that already served, the answer is likely to be that it isn't safe to turn a man with Ezra's record out without parole supervision. If we try the court method, asking for a reversal, endless time—and money—would have to be spent before Ezra could go free. So we—the sponsoring committee and our lawyers—think the best thing to do is just to ask that Ezra be put back on parole, as he was when he was sent up. It gets Ezra out quickest, and it reassures Kansas that he'll be supervised by their officers for as long as, perhaps, eight years."

When I saw that Ezra had more than fifty sound business and professional men on his side at the hearing, I was sure that Prentice Townsend, the pardons and parole attorney, would quietly let Ezra return to parole. But I was wrong. Mr. Townsend ducked the issue. He heard the proposal and the arguments for it quietly and with courtesy. Then he ruled that it was a matter for the board of paroles to treat as a clemency plea rather than for him to decide on a legal basis.

So we all went over to the building where the state parole board was sitting. The twenty of us who were admitted to their chamber filled it.

Rue Holland spoke first. It seemed to me that the board members were listening with a sort of icy courtesy that barely masked their hostility. Perhaps I was prejudiced. Rue spoke quietly, and to the point. When he finished, Jim Post and some of Ezra's other friends there gave character espousals of Ezra. Then Rue asked me to speak. I reminded the board that Warden Duffy and Warden Crouse had both written them in favor of Ezra's parole, and that Sherman Crouse, in all his years as a prison official, had never before sent a letter to the board on behalf of a prisoner.

That should have been enough. I waited for the members to say something, or even to nod. But they just sat there, still polite, still icy, still noncommittal. So I pulled out a packet of letters Ezra had written me, told the board members what they were and selected one to read out loud.

Ezra had written:

To begin with, Bill, there is no quick cure-all or panacea for what ails us, no light we can turn on in our minds or anywhere else that will give us instant illumination of the truth, no walls we can tear down or doors we can open that will let us arrive, instantly, at the truth of what ails us, nor the cure for that ailment. But there is a way to leave all of our past behind us and to build a solid future. That way is to change and grow.

Grow up out of the habits and ruts of ignorance and crime; grow up and away from jealousy and hate; grow out of immaturity and greed.

To change and grow up to be men; to place our feet firmly on the ground and face up to life and to our responsibilities; to do our own thinking for a change, instead of letting the people around us do our thinking for us.

To do this there is one thing we must have. That one thing is faith. We must believe in ourselves. This is one thing that we who break the law have never had. The faith that we need in ourselves and in our abilities to achieve the success and position in life that we want or think we should have.

We have let this weakness, or this lack of faith, drive us from one heartbreak to another—and on to mistake after mistake—until we reach the lowest point in our miserable existence.

I finally believe in and have faith in other people, not just the people outside but also the people in here too, the guys, the guards, my prison committee, and the people I deal with every day—in other words, humanity. And now, finally, I am a part of the world. Just a little part, but at least I am a part.

I have finally stopped living beneath everything on the underside, in the smoke, the slime and the neon lights and the darkness. Instead of underworld I am in the upper-world for a change, way on top where it is light and where I can breathe friendly air and where there are smiles and laughter instead of snarls and curses. For this, I thank God.

"Those, gentlemen," I said, "are the innermost thoughts of Ezra Kingsley, the man for whom this group of responsible citizens seeks relief. We believe that Ezra Kingsley ought to be put in a position where he will be eligible for parole, which you gentlemen will finally decide upon. However, it is necessary first for the inequity in the way he is serving his sentence to be corrected. This you have the power to do."

When I finished, the chairman thanked us for our trouble and said we would, in due course, hear from the board. He asked not a single question.

Ten days later I got a wire from Ezra Kingsley. He had been turned down cold. The board had sent for him, inter-

viewed him for seventeen minutes—without ever asking him
to tell them his own present attitude—and had then refused
him.

The fact that Clinton Duffy, a penologist of such high
standing, had found Ezra worth a two-hour interview—after
which he had concluded that there was no need or use in keeping Ezra Kingsley in prison any more—should have influenced
the board into at least spending a little more time with Ezra.

My reaction was anger. Then I got a letter from Ezra:

> It has been one whole week since I received my denial notice
> from Topeka and I still haven't snapped back to normal yet,
> but I am looking at things a lot more clearly than I did the
> first few moments.
>
> How in the world can a man like me, who has never had
> a real friend in my entire life, complain because something
> didn't go my way? Friends like you, Bill, and all of the oth-
> ers who tried to help make me realize how truly fortunate I
> am to have people who will always care about what happens
> to Ezra Kingsley.
>
> I am not bitter. I am not bitter because in reality it has
> been a good lesson to me. It makes me see just how far it is
> from what I was to what I am now—and how far I have yet
> to go. The gulf between then and now keeps widening and I
> have found that I can't go back even if I wanted to.
>
> This, from the incorrigible Ezra Kingsley.

Topeka, capital city of Kansas, wanted a Seventh Step
Club, where ex-prisoners could legally congregate and help
each other to go straight. Mayor Charles W. Wright, Jr., Chief
of Police Dana L. Hummer, and other officials wanted it. This
was a significant step not only for ex-prisoners in Topeka but

also for Seventh Step, since the Kansas capital was the meeting place of the board of parole.

Every Seventh Step Foundation program is, of course, headed by an ex-convict. The man who was chosen as the director of the Topeka project was a charter member of my very first prerelease class—the one that composed the Seven Steps to Freedom. Bill Larson is a many-time loser. As a matter of fact, the longest period of time that he had been able to maintain his freedom without a warrant for his arrest in the last twenty years was three days. His first job when he got out of Lansing was as janitor at the Seventh Step Club in Kansas City. At first he refused to leave the premises. Like Pegleg, Wayne Bethea, and so many other men who have spent much of their lives in prison, he found the street terrifying.

He maintained his freedom one day at a time. At first he used to sit in the window and look at the bank across the street—"a real crackerbox" he used to call it—and say that he would refrain from robbing that bank that day. Later, after he had become more firmly adjusted to society, he opened a bank account in that same bank. He still watched it often.

"Now why are you staring at that bank?" I asked him one day.

"Because it's such a damned crackerbox that I want to protect my money," he answered.

It was a modest beginning, but it was a beginning. From that time on, Bill progressed steadily and quickly. I wouldn't have believed it possible for anyone to change so radically if I hadn't seen it with my own eyes. Now, Bill is at home in the company of professional men and their wives. He is welcome at the country club, and he is a highly respected member of his community. Bill continues to head the program he started in Topeka, and he has opened another prerelease class at the

Diagnostic Center. He is also one of the most effective workers Seventh Step has in the field of preventing juvenile delinquency.

Ezra and I were corresponding regularly, about three times
a week. I wrote to him about the Topeka project. I also got
in touch with Tennessee Ernie Ford, who had been so very
sympathetic to the Seventh Step program when I was promoting *My Shadow Ran Fast*. He was scheduled to appear at the
Kansas State Fair in Topeka about the same time as we would
be ready to start the drive for the new club. I asked Tennessee
Ernie to help kick off the drive, and he agreed at once.

And Ezra came up with a brilliant suggestion. Of course,
the men who wanted to join the new Topeka club—ex-convicts
all—would be at the meeting. Ezra wrote:

> Men on the outside who have been away from here for a few
> months are apt to forget how tough it was in prison. They
> are subject to erase it from their minds. Why not take our
> committee, all chained and handcuffed and in their prison
> clothes, to the meeting? I think it would help a lot of guys on
> the outside and it should be the most eloquent way I know
> to tell them how lucky they are, just to have their freedom.

In Topeka a few days later, I visited Chuck McAtee, director of Kansas prisons, and proposed Ezra's plan. McAtee
agreed that a dramatic reminder such as this would be worth
trying.

Press, radio, television, boomed the meeting in advance, and
showed up to cover it. It seemed, too, that every city official and
most of the state officials were there, too. The meeting was held
in what would be the new clubrooms when money was raised to
rent and furnish them. Clement Stone had offered to meet half

the budget if the people of Topeka would raise the other half. It looked as though they would. There were several hundred people jammed into the rooms, more than a hundred of them ex-prisoners, graduates of the prerelease class at Lansing.

Ex-convicts, sponsoring squarejohns, public officials, philanthropists, and plain lion-hunters who wanted to meet Tennessee Ernie were all there. Ernie himself was still working at the state fair when Ezra and his committee arrived from Lansing—in chains. The men shuffled into the room awkwardly, in single file, and stood patiently for inspection.

Then the guard who had brought them from Lansing removed the irons, and left them lying on the floor in grim piles, one for each committeeman.

Recognizing former prison mates, Ezra called to them by name. Then he stood before them and said, "I know every one of you guys, and every one of you knows me. In prison, you used to look up to me. You thought I was a big wheel. How do I look to you now, dressed in my prison clothes? Would you like to imitate me now? Perhaps trade places?"

There was silence as Ezra bent to pick up the chains and manacles at his feet. Holding them in his fist over his head, he rattled them vigorously and continued, "This is the way I got here. In chains. You guys arrived here in outside clothes and in cars. When we leave here tonight I'll still be in chains. Every one of you guys knows what the cell looks like that I'll sleep in—after they have me securely locked up again! Well, these chains will fit you too. There are two ways you can go back to that prison as Lansing. One of them is to go back as a success, dressing in outside clothes, for the purpose of talking to the class and helping some guy face the truth about himself. The other way is in chains. That's the way Ezra Kingsley, 'the big wheel,' is going back tonight. In chains. Think it over."

It was a dramatic summary of what Seventh Step stands for, and every ex-convict in the room was impressed.

When Tennessee Ernie arrived, he went straight to Ezra and the other men in prison gray and said, "You guys are the ones I want to see. Let's go some place where we can talk." And with that, he took them off into one of the smaller clubrooms, shut the door, and didn't come out for an hour.

When he did, he was the usual, obliging performer. He shook hands with officials and wealthy men who could do Seventh Step some good, gave interviews, broadcast on both radio and TV for the foundation. The budget was raised.

Ezra wrote me about how he felt, standing in chains and being stared at as though he were in a zoo. "When I looked at the faces around me, all I knew for sure was that I was going to help some of those guys on parole to stay out."

And about the trip back to Lansing.

When we first started back, I never saw lights so bright nor people so happy. But as we neared the prison it seemed that every time the car went over an expansion crack in the highway the noise said Lan, and the singing of the tires hitting the cracks said sing, Lan . . . sing, Lansing . . . Lansing. As we came closer I got smaller and the chains got heavier until they weighed a ton. When we turned the corner from the highway to the joint, I wanted to scream. I have relived the trip over at least one hundred times, and because I know it helped, I can hardly wait for the next one. Will there be one?

Chapter 19

A note from Clement Stone started us packing again.

> Bill, it has been called to my attention that over ten percent of the nation's convicts are in the State of California. That state has a high crime rate and is most receptive to innovations in penology. In view of recent discussions concerning expansion of our program and also since Warden Duffy has joined us, California sounds like an ideal state for our operations. I think you should consider moving there for this purpose. Perhaps this is the right time to open the program in such prisons as San Quentin, Folsom, Chino, etc.

I had waited a long time for the opportunity to walk back into San Quentin as a successful ex-convict. That was where this had all started. I wanted to bring the program to those men, some of whom would probably remember me from the years I served there.

Pony and I had been to California for a short vacation not long before, and knew of a house for sale out on the desert. We bought it by phone, and I flew ahead of Pony and Bonnie for a meeting with the two top prison officials in California, Walter Dunbar, director of the Department of Corrections, and Richard A. McGee, administrator of the Youth and Adults Correction Agency. Warden Duffy also attended the meeting.

I am an ex-convict, and a California ex-convict at that, but those two highly placed California officials proved their open-mindedness by listening intently to what Seventh Step had done back in Kansas. Then they turned us over to Warden Lawrence Wilson of San Quentin and Superintendent E.J. Oberhauser of the California Institution for Men at Chino. These are the principal medium-security and minimum-security penitentiaries for the state.

They were as cooperative as their superiors had been. It was immediately apparent that they were not merely giving lip service to something passed down from above. Anything that would help the men in their charge was something in which they were interested.

Duffy and I talked things over and decided to bring Joe Wallace west from Chicago to start a prerelease class at Chino. Karl Bowen moved up to Cook County from Lansing, and Tim Sullivan, another ex-convict, stepped in at Lansing. For the one at San Quentin, Duffy suggested an ex named James O'Toole, whom I had not met before.

James John Vincent Patrick O'Toole is a handsome six-footer in his mid-forties. Jim's thick dark hair is graying just enough to give him a look of distinction, and the expression in his dark brown eyes has a directness that compels attention. He is a well-educated man and extremely articulate.

Jim O'Toole and I had something in common. His father had been an attorney, mine a judge—and we had both done time. But Jim had long since given up forging checks, as I had given up armed robbery, and he looked like a good bet for Seventh Step. We sent him east to Lansing for six weeks of training by Ezra Kingsley.

There was space behind our house in Palm Desert for an office. We had it built. Then I hired a secretary and went to work.

California has one advantage over most places; it is full of show business people, always generous about giving their time and money and lending their names to anything that will make the world a little better. Tuffy Goff, who played Abner for so many years on the radio, was a nearby neighbor whom Tennessee Ernie had asked to look me up. He introduced us to the rest of our neighbors. Through him we also met Alice Faye and Phil Harris, who at once asked us to dinner. Phil had read *My Shadow Ran Fast* and wanted to learn more about the program.

The dinner ended up with a date for Phil, Tuffy, and Andy Devine to go to a prerelease class at Chino with me. Before the night came for the class, Larry Storch of the television *F Troop* program agreed to come also.

Chino was not a new experience for me. I had spent the last three months of my sentence there back when the minimum-security installation first opened. But that had been a long time back.

Chino cannot be compared to any other prison in the country. Just for one thing, in its approximate twenty-five years of operation, it has never had a killing. For another thing, Chino has no walls. The current superintendent at Chino, E.J. Oberhauser, will sometimes welcome a group of new arrivals with this kind of speech: "My name is Oberhauser. Most people call me Obie.

"Now, if you decide to run away from here and head south, you're going to run smack into the Maximum Security Diagnostic Center, and it's going to give you a lot of trouble. If you head east, you have nothing in your way at all, but it's a long way to the closest road. If you head north, you can get to a road fairly easily, but there's cattle running out there, and to keep them in we have a barbed-wire fence that's about four feet high, which you have to climb. And if you head west, you go out through all the housing and stuff, so that's a bad way to go. If you climb the fence, you're subject to rip your pants. So, I would suggest that you put your coat over the barbed wire and then use that, climb over the coat.

"Our officers do not carry guns or clubs. So there's nothing to stop you from going but one thing—and that is, if you run away from here, you can never come back again. When they catch you, you'll go to some other prison in California, and that's where you'll do the rest of your sentence. That's the only threat. If you run away, you can't come back."

The Seventh Step committee there, composed of seven men, has a combined record of having served more than a hundred years. The use of Chino is not confined to boys and young men who have made one false step.

While Jim O'Toole was in Kansas for his training, Joe Wallace was setting up a committee and opening the classes at Chino. I was able to judge how thoroughly Joe had done his job when I visited my first Chino class, in company with Phil Harris, Tuffy Goff, and Andy Devine. I felt for all the world as if I were right back in the room at Lansing with Ezra Kingsley presiding. The committee functioned smoothly and effectively, the convicts who took the podium were facing the same problems as those in Lansing, and the men in the class tore at them with the same barrage of truth-revealing questions.

The surest way to gain a friend for Seventh Step work is to take a guest to one of our prison classes. We gained three friends that night. In the latter part of the program, when Phil, Andy, and Tuffy were asked to speak, they told the men so in no uncertain terms.

The Lansing class was now known all over the country, both by the public and by penologists. The chiefs of police of both Kansas Cities—Clarence M. Kelley of Missouri and T. B. Peacock of Kansas—had not only been to the Seventh Step Club, but had written endorsing the work wholeheartedly. So had the mayor of Kansas City, Kansas, Joseph H. McDowell, and the lieutenant governor of Kansas, John W. Crutcher. Mr. Crutcher wrote:

It has been my good fortune to have an opportunity to observe the splendid work being done by the Seventh Step Foundation in Kansas City, Kansas. In my opinion, this project represents American initiative at its best. Without benefit of financial help or prodding from the Federal Government, the State Government, or government at any level, dedicated people have undertaken to do something to correct a great area of social need.

I know that this project has already saved the State of Kansas hundreds of thousands of dollars, and it is only an infant program. The potentialities are truly unlimited.

I am pleased to offer you my wholehearted congratulations, for the work done thus far. Furthermore, if I can be of any assistance to you in furthering the good work being done, I suggest that you call on me to help.

Not long afterward I received another letter that pleased me no end. This one came for the famous Dr. Karl Menninger of the Menninger Foundation, a psychiatrist who has a deep interest in the problem of crime. Dr. Menninger read *My Shadow*, and he asked me to visit his foundation to tell the staff about our program. I was tied up at the time, and so was Joe Wallace, so I asked Bill Larson of our Topeka program to go on behalf of the Seventh Step Foundation. Bill gave the psychiatrists and psychologists a graphic picture of our work and the philosophy behind it, and Dr. Menninger reacted with an enthusiasm that surprised me. He sent members of his staff to visit Seventh Step classes and took a lively interest in their reports. In his letter to me, he said:

> I think this may do more good to change the attitude of the public toward the ridiculous, futile techniques they are now using in the jail system than anything else that has happened.

The delay and stalling about Ezra's release irked me. I am not the most patient of men. I toyed with the idea of publicizing the frustrations we were encountering, because Ezra's case seemed to me typical of the kind of injustice Kansas was tolerating. It would be a dramatic example of the attitude that had hindered Seventh Step work from the beginning. But I was afraid that any public uproar I raised might be costly—not for the authorities, that is, but for Ezra. I asked him if he knew what would happen if I cited him—on the air, in the papers—as a typical victim of injustice.

"Yes," he said calmly, "twelve more years."

"Rough years, Ezra. It would be open season on Ezra Kingsley."

He shrugged. "It's my decision to make, Bill. I'll write you in a day or so."

Three days later I got a letter. Let it speak for itself.

There's no such thing as easy time, Bill. All of the time I have done has been hard. I want you to know that I am for whatever you want to do that will help our program nationally and that will help other men to change their lives. If you think you can help the program around the country by tearing into Kansas and using my case as an example, then shoot your best stick—I'll be standing by to chalk your cue.

Ezra could take it, but I couldn't. Anyway, by that time I had cooled off. The foundation was doing so well around the country that it didn't need a human sacrifice in the shape of Ezra Kingsley. It was worth a lot more to the work, and to me, for Ezra to get out.

The break came. Melvin M. Belli read *My Shadow* and liked it. The colorful nationally famous San Francisco lawyer wrote me a letter which ended, "If I can ever be of any help to you, just let me know."

Could he be of help? I almost knocked the telephone over grabbing it. Modern communication is pretty wonderful. Within a few minutes we were calling each other Mel and Bill, and I was asking him if he really meant what he said.

Four days later he and I were on our way to Kansas. Lansing, first. Mel wanted to meet Ezra. They were alone in the chaplain's office for quite a while. Then they came out, arm in arm, with the lawyer saying "It looks like I have a new nonpaying client" in a hearty tone of self-congratulation.

Mel Belli's activities never go unnoticed. Kansas knew he was at Lansing, and the class that night was packed with prisoners and squarejohns. Lieutenant Governor Crutcher was there, and so were Warden Crouse, Kansas Director of Prisons McAtee, and former Governor Payne Ratner.

Through the first hour, as Ezra conducted the program, he took a good deal of kidding about the day being his fortieth birthday—the usual sort of thing about growing a white beard and calling himself Gramps.

Then he turned the rostrum over to his new attorney. Mel Belli, in turn, introduced former Governor Payne Ratner of Kansas and Lieutenant Governor Crutcher, Warden Crouse, and Mr. McAtee to the mike, organized them into a quartet, and boomingly—Belli-style—led them in singing Happy Birthday to Ezra.

Mel may have wondered why the applause was delayed. It was something that only a convict or an ex-con would have known. The men were dumbfounded at seeing such a distinguished group honoring a prisoner. When they did applaud, it was thunderous. Mel Belli stood up there, beaming until he got absolute silence. Then he turned to the other members of his quartet and said, "Gentlemen, you've just sung Happy Birthday to a man who has done more for his prison than any convict in history. He doesn't have anything to be happy about. What about you, gentlemen? Are you happy or proud of yourselves for keeping this man locked up?"

Ezra's elbow gently dug into my ribs as he whispered, "Hey, buddy, that's my lawyer!"

Mel got a Kansas attorney, Dave Carson, to work with him, and set about building up a plea to have Ezra's illegal sentence set aside. I went back to the desert pretty certain that we would soon have Ezra out.

I was happy until I got back to Palm Desert. Pony and I had been having what the experts call "marital difficulties" for some time. We had tried to resolve them in the past, but this time we had to agree to separate.

It appears to be fashionable these days to "confess all" about marital troubles, cover pages and pages with intimate details of fights, misunderstandings, drunken rages and the like. Such "confessions" repel me. Some things should remain private. Even a very brief account I will find painful to render, but that much I owe my reader.

The trouble had started way back in Kansas City. Pony was as involved in my prison work as I. She was dedicated to it and she worked at it. I don't know how I could have begun the Seventh Step without her tremendous help.

Pony, however, had suffered an experience far more traumatic than anything I had gone through. She had witnessed her best friend's execution. I have never been sure whether my work in prisons, where I took her along whenever possible, might not have been intolerably painful for her. I never even considered the possibility until it was too late.

And I'm sure I am not the easiest guy in the world to live with—as maybe the reader has guessed. I tend to be very emotional and I live an intense life—sometimes I work twenty hours at a stretch and then collapse. In pursuit of an immediate goal I will pack my bags and fly three thousand miles at a moment's notice. I come back when the job is done. All this is hard on a wife. And I'm sure I wasn't always considerate of Pony's feelings.

In any event, Pony is remarried now—to a man who did time with me in San Quentin. He is very active in the rehabilitation of alcoholics, and so is Pony. She needs a full schedule and some work she cares about deeply to make her happy. I hope she is.

When Pony and I separated, I tried to lose myself in my involvement with the Seventh Step program.

Of course I was corresponding regularly with Ezra, and he asked me if I'd use my show business connections to get Lansing some Thanksgiving Day entertainment. I called Phil Ford and Mimi Hines first.

Mimi let out a yelp when she heard what I wanted. She explained that it wasn't going to be easy to be in Lansing on the twenty-fifth. "We don't close here in Chicago till the twenty-third. The next day Decca has a recording session set up. Okay, we have Thanksgiving Day off, but it's the only one. Decca needs us again on the twenty-sixth. And on the twenty-seventh, rehearsals start in New York for *Funny Girl*. We were planning on that day off for the only rest we're going to get for a long, long time. How important is this Lansing show?"

"Real important," I said. "But if you can't make it, I'll certainly understand."

Sounds of a conference on the other end of the line came to me. Then Mimi came back on. "Phil says hello, and we'll be there Thanksgiving. See you in prison, huh?"

So I got a show for Ezra, and in so doing, I almost signed his death warrant.

Phil and Mimi arrived in Kansas City late the night before Thanksgiving. When we arrived in the prison the next day, Ezra and his committee escorted us from the front gate to the auditorium. The audience was already assembled, and the musicians Phil and Mimi had brought set up their instruments immediately. I walked out on stage within minutes after we arrived. I told a few opening jokes and then I introduced Phil and Mimi and went offstage to relax. I was surprised to see that Ezra was still backstage. He was sitting on a saw horse with his arms crossed over his chest. I sat down beside him and asked, "What are you doing back here? Why aren't you out front watching the show?"

"I will be. Just give me a minute or two."

"Something's wrong, isn't it, Ezra?"

Ezra didn't answer, but the tight expression on his face was answer enough.

"Spill it, buddy," I said.

Ezra turned it over in his mind. His face didn't change, but he was obviously pondering. "Okay," he said. "I guess so. Bill, a couple of guys are getting set to kill me. Today. During the show."

Ezra can be funny, but this was not his brand of kidding. I kept my voice quiet, but I certainly didn't feel calm. "What did you do to them?"

"It's a nutty story," Ezra said. "They want to kill me because Phil Ford and Mimi Hines showed up today."

"What?"

"It's simple," Ezra said. "When I told the men that Phil and Mimi were going to be here on Thanksgiving Day, one of the wise guys in the joint saw a chance to make some money. He had some sort of show business paper saying that Phil and Mimi were tied up with recording dates in Chicago till they were due for rehearsals in New York, so he figured they'd cancel out here. He and his brother started making book against the show going on."

"Did you cover their bets?"

"Hell, no," Ezra said. "I gave up gambling. You know that. But you know my rep in this joint. A lot of men bet the show would go on just because I said so. There's been as many bets laid as usually go down on a world series. The brothers got clipped, bad, and they blame me. So . . ." He spread his hands and shrugged.

"That's crazy."

"Who says all the guys in this joint are sane? Hell, Bill, you've done time, and you know some of the screwy little reasons guys get killed. You've been through it yourself."

"What are you going to do about it?"

He gave another shrug and looked at me with a wry grin.

"Before you and your damn Seven Steps came along, I'd have killed them or had them killed. I guess that's out now, though."

"So what *will* you do?"

We both knew there wasn't a safe spot in the prison for him. If he didn't go out into the audience, he'd get it in the mess hall, the infirmary, a corridor, or even in his cell at night.

Ezra snorted, and laughed a little. "Hell, I don't expect to get killed," he said. "I'm going out there, and walk right down the aisle to where they're sitting. I'm going to give them one shot at my back. Just one. I've got friends all around them who will see to it they don't get a chance for a second cut."

"Big deal! Suppose one cut is all they need."

"Come on, Bill, you know better than that. It hardly ever happens that one cut kills anyone. I don't think it's going to happen to me."

Before I could think of an answer to that one, the convict who was acting as stage manager came up to me. "Hey, Bill," he said, "didn't you hear Mimi give you your cue? You're supposed to be onstage."

Ezra gave me a friendly shove and said, "You're on, buddy. Don't worry about me."

That was easier said than done. I walked out onstage and took my place between Phil and Mimi. Mimi handed me the mike, and I was trembling so I could hardly hold it. We went into the brief routine that we had rehearsed in their hotel suite the night before. As we worked, I saw Ezra's white-clad figure appear from the wings.

He walked to the back of the audience, and then came down the left aisle. About ten rows from the back he stopped, braced his shoulders, and folded his arms across his chest again—a typical Ezra Kingsley stance.

The mike slipped in my clammy hand and almost got away from me. I brought my left hand up to help me hold on. The prisoners around Ezra's part of the audience had stopped laughing. The rest of the men couldn't see what was going on.

Cue line, feed line, gag line. I was working precisely from rehearsed memory. I could no longer tell if anybody in the audience was responding.

This couldn't go on. It didn't. After just a couple minutes Ezra turned around, bent over two men in the audience, and said something. And then the men around him were laughing. A couple of minutes later, my small part of the show was over and I was backstage, Mimi was singing, and Ezra was there again sitting on the same sawhorse, watching intently and totally relaxed. I sat down.

"What the hell happened, buddy?" I said.

"Shhh!" he said. "Watch the show."

"The show!" I exploded. "What happened out there?"

"Nothing happened. The guys are eating this show up. I guess my bookie friend looked around and figured the odds a little different. It's not them against me, it's them against eighteen hundred cons who give me credit for getting this show in here. It's a great show, too, so why don't you dummy up and let me watch it?"

Ezra was right. It was a great show. Sitting side by side on the crude backstage sawhorse, my friend and I enjoyed every minute of it. At the end, Mimi finished as she had in the Cook County jail, trailing the mike cord and going down into the audience alone to sing "People."

Once she began, the same awed hush descended over the cons that she had evoked in Cook County. As she sang about how very lucky people who need people are, Ezra turned to me and grinned. "Ain't it the truth," he said.

Lansing had never relaxed its rule against having women visitors inside the walls, and we always found that rule a hindrance to our work. When a man has served a long sentence in a completely masculine environment, he finds it very difficult to adjust to the outside world, where half the population happens to be composed of women. We had approached Crouse many times to ask for permission to bring women to the prerelease class, but he—like most wardens of men's penitentiaries—feared that the presence of women would precipitate an incident.

After the show Mimi had given, I went to see Crouse again, hoping that the reception she had enjoyed—which was almost reverent—might convince him that women could safely attend our classes. He was still not convinced. But he did give me permission to have the sponsors bring their wives to the Seventh Step anniversary dinner which he had arranged for the prerelease class and committee. He brought Mrs. Crouse to the dinner, too. It was the first time she had ever been inside the prison.

A committeeman who ran the class bulletin at the time wrote up the anniversary dinner:

The humming of conversation drones in your ears, and you hear yourself making polite conversation with your guest, conscious of your manners at all times, and hoping that you won't, from a terrible habit, slip with a swearword that comes so natural in your everyday conversation in prison, because of the embarrassment it would cause you and your guest. Yet you know down deep, the embarrassment would really be more on your side, because your guest would realize you didn't mean it, and it would be more amusing to them than anything else.

Those unbelievable sounds, so familiar, taking you back in memory. The laughter of the women sitting all around you. If you were to close your eyes and listen, familiar incidents, familiar sounds, the smell of perfume . . . all so real . . . and yet so unreal. Then if you were to open your eyes you know that this is real, but only for a few hours, and you don't want to waste one minute, you don't want to miss anything, you want to take everything in . . . and you do. A woman touches you on the hand to get your attention, and you pull back as if you were shocked with an electric stick . . . and you glance around to see if some guard or someone has seen this sudden movement, and misinterpreted the meaning. Shy? Nervous? I hope to tell you! You have the feeling for just a little while of being free, and how nice it would be to just get up and walk out with the crowd.

Then suddenly . . . it's all gone! You're in your cell, it's dark, the bull is making the 3:00 a.m. count, and in the shadows, on the bench, you can see the menus laying there . . . so you know it happened . . . because you can't sleep. The best evening you ever had in prison . . . but it's over . . . and you're in prison!

Chapter 20

The new programs in California were a dream come true, for me and for everyone who had put so much into the Seventh Step for so long. Finally, expansion to a national scale was not a mere hope but a secure reality. All of us visualized swiftly branching out into one prison after another, and through it meant more work than we had ever had before, it was just what we wanted.

And then, without warning, Seventh Step suddenly faced the worst crisis since its inception. The crisis occurred when an expected pledge of a substantial sum, which we had considered basic to our plans, did not materialize. Our financial margin was always thin at best. Every cent we had available went into solidifying our gains and expanding. So the loss of this pledge was a disaster. Suddenly our plans were all daydreams. Only now they were daydreams we had held out as realities to the men at Chino and San Quentin as well as Lansing and Cook

County, and we had no funds to support even one of these pre-release programs, let alone four.

In the confusion that followed this development, a well-meaning organization that had an honest regard for our intentions but no understanding at all of our basic principles offered to solve all our problems by taking over the foundation and replacing the ex-convicts on our board of directors with professional social workers and other respectable, educated people. When we failed to show enthusiasm, I'm afraid their feelings were hurt. But even so, they kindly offered me a handsome salary for life to take on a strictly figurehead position helping them out with public relations. When I declined, they made an even more handsome offer to Warden Duffy. He didn't care to go into P.R. work either, as it turned out.

This episode finished our hopes for receiving a sum of money substantial enough to meet our projected budgets. The prerelease class leaders, the Seventh Step Club managers, the secretaries, everyone who had agreed to work for the salaries we had projected, would have to be told there were no salaries at all. They were duly informed, and what followed was perhaps the greatest miracle of the whole program.

Nobody quit.

I suppose we shouldn't have been surprised where the ex-convicts were concerned. One of our main preoccupations when we'd screened them was to make certain they were all solid. And when things went badly, they stayed solid.

The Chicago program is the only one that closed for lack of funds. Karl Bowen, however, continues to help convicts and ex-convicts. He has joined an organization in South Carolina that is very similar to Alcoholics Anonymous but concentrates on men in trouble with the law. It isn't the Seventh

Step Foundation, but it was the best Karl could do under the circumstances.

The Kansas program at Lansing began to founder badly when Tim Sullivan—whom we call Old Faithful—suffered a heart attack. Tim worked as a heavy equipment operator all day, but he still managed to attend every committee meeting and every prerelease class and to show up at the outside club every day, until the strain became too much for him and ruined his health. Joe Wallace immediately moved back to Kansas to take over the program in the state in which we had started.

Bill Hanks, a former armed robber whom Jim O'Toole knew well, agreed to take over the Chino program without even the promise of a salary. Jim himself, after months of strain as the Seventh Step state director for California, suffered a mild stroke. His doctors told him to take it easy, but he was too dedicated and refused. The effects of the stroke are only slightly noticeable. One side of his handsome face is partially paralyzed, but he has largely controlled the paralysis by a massive application of will.

Bob Kale, a man who had served time in both San Quentin and Folsom and who had successfully maintained his freedom for more than fifteen years, had been working with Jim on a part-time volunteer basis. When the financial crisis hit us, Bob went to work full time and took over the program at San Quentin to relieve Jim of some of his responsibilities. In his fifteen years of freedom Bob had managed to build up a savings account. More than once since he went off salary to help us, he has given some of his modest savings to fellow workers who had nothing at all.

Bill Larson—who was once too frightened of the street to leave the Kansas City clubroom—became a public speaker and earns his livelihood that way. He continues his work with juveniles and with the Diagnostic Center in the Topeka chapter.

Among the men who had been out long enough to have made a secure place for themselves and their families, some sold their homes, or took out second mortgages if they could get them, and even sold their cars and rode a bus out to the prisons. The people who had never been in prison stayed by us too, and the work went on.

Nowadays almost all our programs are self-supporting. The ones that aren't—those that are getting started—soon will be self-supporting. In San Francisco, funds are supplied by an outfit that used to be called the Saints and Sinners, which raised money for the Shriners' Milk Fund. When it had raised enough for that cause, it began to fall apart. Jim O'Toole got the men reorganized into a new luncheon group called the Squarejohns. They raffle off a Rolls Royce once a year—five hundred tickets at a hundred dollars a ticket. They hold a monthly luncheon, just for fun, which shows a profit. This is turned over to Jim for Seventh Step work at San Quentin and in the San Francisco clubhouse. Some of our people have gone around and collected stuff people didn't want and put on white elephant auctions at county fairgrounds. Kansas gets fine support from a Topeka committee that includes the chief of police and the mayor of the capital of Kansas.

And so on. We never have enough money to open in all the places we're needed, but we try to get along.

Our people, almost without exception, made more money before they joined the movement. Joe Wallace is only one example. Even when he drew a salary from the foundation, it was a much smaller one than he had had from General Motors. Our workers care very little about money, obviously.

But the foundation needs more money, on a national basis, to start new programs. Eventually we hope to have a revolving fund that will start programs and then demonstrate their success to local people, who are more likely to take over a successful project than an untried one.

At this time, there are active Seventh Step chapters in San Jose, Los Angeles, San Francisco, Sacramento, Oakland, Kansas City, and Topeka. Some three thousand five hundred convicts who attended Seventh Step classes are maintaining their freedom. But there is still a great deal of work to be done. There are more than three hundred thousand men in prisons in this country.

The pressure of our financial crisis also told on the men on the committees inside the prisons. But in every penitentiary, men can be found who are as solid and as strong as Ezra Kingsley, and able to do everything he had done. As I am writing this, I can name five men who either are or have been coordinators of prerelease classes who have the same kind of background and strength. They are: Rick Clutchey, the first coordinator at San Quentin; Red Gay, the present coordinator at San Quentin; Russ Olin, the first coordinator at Chino; Willie Bykes, the present coordinator at Chino; and Bob Reeves, at Lansing.

The efforts Seventh Step put into Lansing are, to our great satisfaction, bearing fruit quite aside from the program's main objective of helping men to maintain their freedom. Although conditions in the penitentiary have not changed materially, a constant effort at improvement is being made. The old solitary "jail" has been torn down but unfortunately it was replaced by a new forbidding place of solitary confinement. A new vocational-training building has been erected, the old benches in the mess hall have been replaced with tables, the tear gassing of inmates has ceased, and physical brutality is almost totally eliminated. Even Sadie has shown signs of great change. He is a booster of the Seventh Step work, and he chose a Seventh Step dinner as the time that he would bring his wife into the prison for the first time.

One area in which we are interested, but has so far done very little, is women's penitentiaries. In women's prisons, the population respects the same qualities of loyalty and strength that male convicts admire, but they are not often found. There are exceptions to every rule, of course, and some of the Seventh Step Foundation's best workers are women ex-convicts. One who comes to mind is Jeanette Cooke, an attractive, statuesque lady who did her time in the fair state of Florida. Jeanette was no shoplifter, either. Her crimes included arson and burglary. She worked with two male confederates, and when the trio was captured, they both turned state's evidence and left Jeanette to ride the beef. In prison she was as solid as any convict, but she did a little thinking and decided to straighten herself out.

When she got out, Jeanette got a job in a fishshed, chopping the heads off the day's catch, splitting them, and scaling them. It was a strange occupation for an attractive girl, but Jeanette didn't mind. She saved her wages and went to night school, took a course in bookkeeping, and eventually got a job in an accountant's office. Then she went on to take night courses at a university until she earned a degree in accounting. She was well on her way to becoming a CPA when she saw me talking about Seventh Step on the Linkletter show.

She began to wonder if working for Seventh Step wasn't what she wanted to do. She went down to a bookstore to get a copy of my first book, and walked out when she found out it cost five dollars. But when she saw me on a second TV show, she decided it might be worth even five dollars, so she bought a copy and read it. Then she wrote to me asking if there was any place in the program for a female ex-con.

At the time I was in Chicago, and I was up to my neck in work. I suggested that she go to Kansas and talk to Miriam Phillips, whom everybody calls Mom, the warden of the Kansas women's prison. Jeanette had worked very hard to qualify for the job she was doing, and it was a good job, but she resigned without a moment's hesitation and did as I had suggested.

Mom Phillips is a California-trained penologist and one of the very best wardens now working, a real Duffy-grade person. She is one of my best friends. One evening, when I was making a speech and saw her sitting in the front row, I pointed to her and said, "That good-looking lady, believe it or not, is a warden. I wish she had been my warden when I was doing time." The audience laughed, and Mom Phillips stood up and replied, "If I had been, you wouldn't be out yet."

Mom and Jeanette hit it off, and our first woman's prerelease class got underway. But despite Mom and Sherman Crouse and a few enlightened state officials, Kansas is still hard to work in, and Jeanette's prerelease class there foundered. She had every right to be discouraged, even to give up. But Jeanette is not a quitter. She now works with us in California.

Jeanette Cooke is not the only worker who was attracted to Seventh Step through a television show. Around the time that the Chino program opened, a woman named Fran Trotten was watching the Art Linkletter show when he was interviewing me about the Seventh step program. Mrs. Trotten is a sweet, motherly woman who has never committed a crime in her life. But her husband, Tom, was a professional forger and had done a couple of stretches in prison. At the time of my appearance on the Linkletter show, he was out on parole and so far, hadn't been violated. But he was having trouble making enough money to support them, and he'd just told his wife he intended to resume his old criminal career.

It's a rare thing for a convict to have a wife who remains loyal to him through a prison term, but Fran loved her husband very deeply. When she heard him say he was going back on the take, it just about broke her heart. When he told her his plans, she was so upset she even threatened to leave him if he carried them out, hoping that would influence him.

Tom wasn't home when his wife saw me on television, but as soon as he came in, she told him all about it. She begged him to at least buy my book and read it to see whether what I was talking about made any sense to him. He agreed to do that much, and when he'd read the book he found he was interested enough to make a point of hearing me next time I was on television. It wasn't long before Linkletter invited me back, and this time Tom Trotten was in my audience. As it happened, I talked about the new Chino program that night. After the show Tom made up his mind to go out to Chino from Pasadena, where he was living, and see whether Seventh Step could help him.

Joe Wallace was running the program at the time. When Tom came in to see him, it was pretty obvious that Tom thought he'd had an awful run of luck and expected sympathy. He started talking about the trouble he was having holding a job and supporting his family. Joe gave him a typical Seventh Step reply.

"You're a phony," Joe said. "You're not trying to maintain your freedom, you're just looking for a free ride. If your freedom is worth anything to you, you'd do anything including starve before you'd go back on the take. I don't believe you're even trying to work. You're not so badly off—you've got education, you're in good health. You should hear some of the troubles the other men have, and they manage to get along without breaking the law, without infringing on the rights of others."

None of this was what Tom thought he wanted to hear, but he took it well. Like most of our men, he recognized the truth about himself when he heard it. And he was sufficiently tired of doing time to take what Joe told him seriously. Once Joe was able to make him admit that he needed to change himself, helping him was easy. Joe was able to get him a steady job at a used car agency, and in only a short while Tom Trotten went from needing help to stay free to giving help to other men. First he went out to visit the Chino classes once in a while, just to show the men who hadn't been released yet that he was out and making it, even though he'd come awfully close to returning to crime. Fran often went too. Chino is quite accessible to female visitors, and she was fascinated by Seventh Step work. After a while, Tom got hooked on the Seventh Step program and began giving free time to helping out on a regular basis. When he finished his parole, he applied for and received authorization from the state to sponsor other ex-cons coming out.

I first heard this story on a visit to Chino one day when Tom and his wife happened to be there. When I told Art Linkletter about it, he was so thrilled to know that one of his TV shows had directly helped a man maintain his freedom that he insisted on having Tom and Fran appear with me. They were happy to oblige. They came on and did a wonderful job of telling their story so that some other ex-con somewhere might benefit from it.

At the end of the show, Art told the audience, "We have given away a great many things on this show over the years—refrigerators, television sets, hifi systems. It makes me proud to know that once, at least, we have given away freedom."

Recently, I had an experience unique in Seventh Step. It began with an invitation from the governor of Tennessee and the warden of the Tennessee State Prison to speak to their men. They assured me I would be completely free to talk about their penitentiary. I went, but with reservations. I expected them to try to involve me in some sort of Operation Whitewash.

Quite the contrary. The warden virtually handed me the keys to the prison. He turned me loose unescorted—told me to go where I wanted to, and see everything there was to be seen. He reiterated that I was free to tell anybody I could persuade to listen to me what I had seen.

I saw plenty. Nearly thirty percent of the guards were illiterate. Overcrowding was as bad as any in the country. And the living conditions were atrocious.

The dinner that night was something. The governor attended, and he, the warden, and the junior chamber of commerce—who sponsored the dinner—had managed to get everyone of importance in the state there. The governor and the warden assured me again that they didn't want me to pull any punches. The warden even gave me a good quote to use in my speech—he said that if the state hired him a professional psychiatrist or psychologist he would use him to treat the guards before starting on the prisoners.

So I told those people just what kind of a hellhole they were keeping their prisoners in. I didn't spare them the cold facts with all the detail I could muster. In the middle of my talk, the commissioner of corrections walked out. But the warden later wrote to me, asked for my autographed picture for his office, and thanked me profusely for helping to call attention to those conditions. The governor made me an honorary colonel on his staff!

The honesty of Tennessee's administration impressed me particularly, because few states are entirely candid about their penological system and its consequences. The official recidivism figures most states publish are a particularly striking case in point.

Some states claim pretty high reform figures, but those who make these claims base them on only their own records of parole violators within the state. Men who have finished their parole and then returned to crime are not included, and neither are multiple offenders arrested and incarcerated outside the state borders.

California is one state that does issue totally honest statistics. It is also the state that has created the most enlightened and successful prison in the country—Chino. Chino's rate of success is much higher than the national average. But even that institution is batting slightly less than .500. The official F.B.I. figures, which—like California's—are perfectly accurate, show a recidivism rate in the neighborhood of 70 percent on a nationwide basis.

Seventh Step is now in its fourth year of operation. We have about four thousand graduates on the street, and our rate of *success* varies somewhere between 85 and 90 percent.

Most of the penologists who still oppose us do so because they see the Seventh Step movement as a threat to their way of life. They are right. They try to justify their position by saying that our work is experimental. The Seventh Step program has been continuously successful since its inception. The experiment has ended, but the work continues.

We do not employ psychiatrists, psychologists, or social workers, much as we respect members of these professions. Convicts may listen politely to educated free men, but they do not answer back. They are not polite at Seventh Step meetings, and they do answer back—because they are deeply involved. The movement is their own.

The Seventh Step program does not demand that members take an active part in reforming others once their own freedom is secure. Unlike Alcoholics Anonymous, we do not impose upon anyone any obligation for another man's success. A great many of our men want to work in the program and we love them for it. A great many move out of Seventh Step as soon as they know they're finished with crime themselves, and we love them too. I think any of our former members would give help willingly if he were asked to in any particular case. But if a man wants to be let alone, we let him alone. Some of our remotivated men find fulfillment in performing social services that have nothing at all to do with crime. A few—though very few—find themselves through religion.

One of these last was a pretty tough boy when I met him, the first night I saw Ezra's committee at work. He is a young handsome fellow and his name is Horace Winger. Horace came from a broken home and when his parents separated, they turned him over to an aunt to be reared. She didn't have much use for youngsters, or so Horace believed, so when he was still in his late teens he left her home and started to make his way in the world as a holdup man. He knocked over service stations in Oklahoma, a liquor store in Kansas, and a bank in Texas. He must have been pretty good at it, because he wasn't caught for quite a long time. When he was caught, it was by accident. He'd committed some minor traffic violation and been stopped by the police. When the officer asked to see his license, Horace opened the glove compartment of his car to get it and there was his gun, in plain sight.

In prison Horace was as tough as they come. He started in Seventh Step the way most prisoners start, as a shuck. But in time he realized that what we had to say made sense, and by the time he was paroled he had decided to stay free. It was at about the same time that Horace found a faith that he felt he could sincerely adopt and live by. His was an unusual choice. A gentile by birth, he became a convert to Judaism. He had never recovered from the shock of his parents' separation and his boyhood loneliness, and he found the sense of family loyalty and closeness among Jews of his acquaintance intensely appealing. Since leaving prison he has married, and he is determined that his children shall enjoy the benefits of a warm family life.

Horace is not working full-time for Seventh Step. He is free, he is not infringing upon the rights of others, and he devotes part of every week to Seventh Step work. If his religion is helping him to do this, then religion is the right solution for him. But it wouldn't be for the vast majority of our men.

It seems to me that the trouble with religion, for most of us, is that the ministers tell us that to be good, we must have faith. But no one has ever told me where faith can be found if one does not happen to have it. If I were to tell a delinquent kid, or a three-time loser to have faith, I would be lost if he asked me how to go about getting it.

For myself, I have thought a great deal about what we call the Power, and when I look back over the long road we have already traveled in Seventh Step, I find a lot to wonder about. I have said before that I am not religious, and I am not. Occasionally, I read the Bible, but I read it with an open mind and not with a determination to take every word as literal truth.

There are a few things I do believe. I believe that Jesus was a very unusual man, but I do not believe that Jesus was the Son of God. To me he was just the Son of Man—a fellow who rebelled against the system, sometimes lost his temper, was loyal to his friends, got tried occasionally, went on working even when he was tired.

At Lansing, the Christmas before last, the class asked me to talk at the Christmas party. Talking to prisoners at Christmastime is about as hard a task as a man can set himself. The time is one of goodwill and hope, family and friends—almost every place but inside bars. There and then, it seems even more so than at other times that the world has forgotten its offenders, locked them away to rot. In those places, just before the New Year starts, hope reaches its lowest level. It is one time when an ordinary break in the routine is not enough. If you say anything, it has to be dead on the level. Or so I thought. So I gave it the best I had.

"Men," I began, "we are all here tonight to celebrate the birthday of a man who lived about two thousand years ago. Most of us have, at one time or another, thought about this guy called Christ. I imagine all of us wish we had an answer.

"I am frank to admit that I don't have an answer . . . that I sometimes envy those men, like your prison chaplain, who have a deep and sincere abiding faith—those men who know they know.

"Tonight I can recite a few simple facts for you, and I am using the words 'simple facts' advisedly. It is, for example, an historical fact that a man named Jesus actually lived some two thousand years ago.

"It is an historical fact that this man lived for only thirty-three years, and that during his entire life he never traveled more than one hundred miles from his home, and that the only words he ever wrote were written in sand. It is an historical fact that the truths this man taught upset the entire Roman empire. It is also an historical fact that this man had a group of followers, now called disciples, but that we, here in prison, might simply call 'his gang.' It is a fact that one of the members of his gang turned stool pigeon for a few pieces of silver. It is a fact that he was convicted by a crooked judge, on what we would call a bum beef. It is a fact that he was sentenced to be executed. And it is a simple fact, an historical fact, that this man, who called himself the Son of God, was nailed onto a cross on which he died a painful death just like any other mortal.

"Now I want to ask you guys to see that story happening in modern times and in language that all of us will understand. Then give some thought to what happened.

"Here we have a man who claimed to be the Son of God, and who, by the working of apparent miracles, had convinced twelve other men that he was indeed the Son of God. Then, one of these guys turned into a stool pigeon and sells out and turns in his leader for a few bucks. And made it stick. The stool pigeon won! He got a crooked judge and he got the leader convicted on a bum beef, and the leader dragged a cross through the streets and finally was nailed to the cross where he painfully bled to death.

"What do you think the reaction of his other followers would be? What would your reaction be if you saw such a thing happen to a leader whom you thought to be invulnerable, immortal, and the Son of God? You, like those eleven faithful followers, would be disappointed. You would be shaken and frightened. The reaction is predictable. The eleven followers ran and hid. Then, three days later, these same frightened eleven men came back into the streets. They claimed the leader had arisen from the dead and they had seen him and eaten dinner with him. Their faith was unshakable. They maintained that story in the face of every conceivable kind of torture and punishment to the point where one of them, called Peter, was about to be crucified in the same manner as his leader. His answer to that was that it was an honor to be crucified in the same manner as his master—so he was crucified upside down.

"In spite of all the pressures and all the ridicule and all the pain, these eleven good guys stood solid, and because they stood solid, we are here tonight to celebrate the birthday of their leader.

"Now let me ask you something. Each of you, perhaps better than people on the outside, knows the workings of a gang. Each of you knows how a group that follows a strong man thinks. Tell me, where would you find eleven men who would forevermore, through every type and kind of pain and torture, adhere to such a tale as they told about a man rising from the dead and having dinner with them? Wouldn't somebody, sometime, finally break? You know damn well they would! But they didn't! Why? Explain it to yourselves, and I think you will find it worthwhile not only to study the life of this man named Jesus, but to try to figure out what it was that this man taught and what it was that this man had that created a kind of strength and loyalty and dedication that the world has never seen before or since. You try to explain it. Simply look at the facts.

"What I think you will ultimately find is that this man taught that there are some spiritual laws that are as immovable as what we now recognize as the physical laws of gravity. I think you will find that he tried to teach them in the only way that the world of that time could understand.

"I do not claim to have the answer. I am here tonight only to set before you those historical facts and ask you simply to investigate them, if you will. Judge for yourselves and, finally, see if there is some application of those facts that you can use in your own lives to create some small miracle of your own. The miracle of freedom.

"Some of you may write off what I have said here tonight as 'too much trouble to investigate' or 'too tough to think about.' Those of you who do that, I pity. Some of you may look on this night as a beginning of thought. Some of you may realize that if that man could accomplish those miracles, then perhaps each of you can create a small miracle of your own freedom and your own happiness. If my words tonight have accomplished that much, then this will, indeed, be a very merry Christmas for me—and for those of you who choose to think.

"This has not been the kind of talk that you have come to expect from me, but those of you who know me best have learned one thing by now, and that is that I will tell you the truth, as I see it, without pulling any punches. I would be less than honest with all of you if I did not give you these thoughts on the eve of the birthday celebration of the man who lived two thousand years ago."

Chapter 21

A week after Christmas I got my best present. Dave Carson, the Kansas lawyer Mel Belli had consulted with, wrote Ezra, and Ezra forwarded the letter to me.

> Dear Mr. Kingsley:
> We appeared in the Butler County District Court. Our motion was sustained, and the Court set aside your sentence and conviction of March 22, 1952.

Ezra was even more terse. He wrote:

> Thank you, buddy.

What the attorney's letter meant was that Ezra's time would be recomputed on the basis of his original sentence, which meant that he should have been eligible for parole three years before. This made it virtually certain that the board of paroles would give Ezra a date for parole. And sure enough, they did—the date was June 1. This was better than nothing, but an awful lot could happen between December 1 and June 1. Any violation, or alleged violation, of prison rules could cancel the parole or delay it.

An awful lot happened to me in those six months. For one thing, I became a father again, after thirteen years. When my first wife and I broke up, Jimmy was only six. Now he was almost nineteen, and had long believed I was dead. His mother and I had decided that was best because of my juvenile and San Quentin record and her hope to remarry.

But *My Shadow Ran Fast* printed my original name—Wilber Power Sewell—which I had changed to Bill Sands when I was entertaining in night clubs. Young Jim Sewell—Boiler Tender James Clinton Sewell, USN—read the book and thought such an unusual name was not likely to belong to two people by coincidence. Besides, he suspected—rightly, as it happens—that his own middle name might have been chosen in honor of Clinton T. Duffy.

He addressed his letter to "Mr. Sands," told me who he was, and said that if I had come up so far in the world that I didn't want to be burdened with a son, he would understand. It wasn't a whining letter. His stepfather, he said, had taught him "to look at every side of the story."

The letter was written aboard ship off the coast of Viet Nam. He wanted to know what his father was really like. At first I thought I knew. I had written a whole book on the subject, and this present book was partly written.

But then, as I wrote Jim—and it was ten days before I could bring myself to start a letter than I didn't tear up—I realized that the book only told what I did, not what I am. And it was the same with all the letters and clippings and tapes of talks in my file.

Jim didn't remember me clearly, but he remembered things I did, like teaching him boxing and taking him and his mother horseback-riding.

Part of my answer to Jim was personal, of course. But part, I think, is worth repeating here because it brought me up against the necessity of having to retake the first step of the Seven. The Step that called for facing myself. I wrote, in part:

I only know that your father is a guy who found himself very late in life (he hopes it wasn't too late) and who thinks of himself as a very fallible guy who is trying as best he knows how, with the tools he has available, to build something that is bigger and stronger and far better than the guy who builds it.

You said in your letter that it was a shock for you to find out who I was and that you "cried like a baby" when you read my name in the book. It was a shock for me, too, to hear from you and I did the same thing!

Then, Jim, you asked me why I left you, my "flesh and blood," and you advanced some theories of your own.

You also told me that you had been taught by your step-father to look at both sides of every question (for which I am grateful) and you asked to hear my side of the story.

Then you said, "Why haven't you ever tried to find me or even write to me once. Please tell me."

The answer to that question, Jim, should be obvious to you. Look at my story! I was the product of a broken home and, I thought, of two parents—neither of whom wanted me. Look at my story, Jim, and you will see the story of a boy who desperately wanted love and who felt that each parent was only using him as a tool with which to hurt the other.

When I was in prison, Jim, I saw the results of far too many broken marriages when each parent was trying to gain the love of the child, while resorting to the very human emotion of trying to discredit the other parent.

I resolved, when I decided to leave your mother, that you would not be put through that particular wringer.

There is no possible way for you to ever know what a decision that was for me to make. There is no possible way for you to ever comprehend how close we were, you and I, from your birth through the first five and a half years of your life.

There is no way for me to tell you that my decision to leave you in the care of your mother and grandparents was based solely and only on a totally non-selfish love for my son. I felt then that I knew what was best for you (no doubt as my father had felt he knew what was best for me) and I have many times since lain awake at night and wondered if I had done the right thing for you because I always knew that for me it was the most heartbreaking and soul-tearing decision that I would ever have to face.

I think I was right, because at age nineteen you are in the Navy, and I was in prison. If it has turned out right for you, Jim, then it has turned out right for me also—because it was for you and because of my love for you that I made that decision.

It may interest you to know that I once drove almost 2,000 miles from Northern California to a little street on the outskirts of Houston, Texas, and sat parked in a car on the corner looking at a little frame house on a street full of tract houses so that I could catch one glimpse of my boy going by as he came home from school.

You asked me to tell you my side of the story. That, Jim, I don't think I can ever do. I can only suggest to you that it sometimes happens that two people get married who are not meant for each other and who bring unhappiness to each other and to those around them. This does not make either person "good" or "bad," it simply means that while they might find happiness elsewhere they cannot find it or bring it to the world with each other.

Perhaps if you could have known me, as others have, during these past years you would know that my decision was based on what I thought to be necessary (and still think so) and that you yourself and my love for you was the ultimate deciding factor. If you had known me during these years as others have known me (and how I wish that were possible) you would also know that I cannot say more than that.

You end your letter by saying you have always loved the father you have never seen but do remember a little and that there is room in your love for me if I will accept it.

I don't know how to answer that. I don't know what to say. I think you must find my answer, Son, in the earlier content of this letter.

I guess I am an emotional guy and because of that I suppose that I had even more dreams and more hopes than most fathers, dreams and hopes of watching my son grow into strong and straight manhood, visions of helping him to find himself and of helping him to form himself. I don't know what part those first six years during which we were so very close together might have played in forming the young man you are today. Naturally, I like to think they have played a large part and every time I hear some learned psychiatrist say that the man's character is all formed in the first six years of childhood I rejoice inside. But I don't know whether to believe it, I only wish I could. I was happy to read you won a trophy for boxing in a Navy smoker because I know at least I started that! I wonder how much more.

What kind of guy am I? I hope you can find at least a part of your answer in the content of this letter.

Why didn't I write to you? I hope you can understand and believe (as you eventually must if you search for the truth because it is true!) that it was because I loved you too much and that of all of the things I have ever done in my life the most courageous thing I have ever done was to try to give you your best chance in life by giving you up.

I would like to know more about you. You have the advantage of reading my life story in a book and I suppose that by now you have figured out for yourself that the reason I did not include you or your mother in my book is the very simple fact that it could serve no useful purpose and could cause nothing but heartbreak and, perhaps, harm.

You, Jim, have the opportunity (if you choose to take it) to get to really *know* me by studying the work that I am doing now and by seeing me through the eyes of the many people who are very close to me and my decisions and this work.

I have no such advantage. I can only get to know you through your letters and by seeing your thoughts expressed in writing. I would like to know much, much, very much more. Tell me more about yourself—what you really think—how you feel inside. Send me pictures by the half-dozen or dozen or more. I want to know you better, need to know you better. I am sure that the young man whom I could get to know would be a young man of whom I could be proud (your first letter certainly said that much!) So write more, Son, a great deal more!

Because whatever "kind of guy" your father is, he most certainly is the kind of guy who wants to hear a great deal more from and about his son.

With love, Bill

In the spring I suddenly got a telegram. Jim was back in the United States, and less than a hundred miles from where I was living. In a matter of hours I met my boy.

I remembered Jim as a lively, active child with the most beautiful eyes and the brightest smile I had ever seen. The young man I met that afternoon was quiet and reserved, but the beautiful eyes were the same, and the smile as bright as ever.

We had only a week together. We water-skied, we rode around beautiful Southern California, we explored things. Most of all, we talked about the present, about the future, and a little about the past.

I had a lot to be thankful for. Jim had not had it too bad. He had got into trouble in the first grade at school for fighting, which was a little like his dad, but he had straightened out as he grew older. He'd finished high school while he was in the Navy, and was only sorry that his grades weren't as high as he felt they could have been if he'd concentrated harder on his studies. But he was a good athlete, and, again like his father, he was fond of sports.

Above all, he is a fine guy, and I am proud of him. After he got back to the Pacific, he wrote me from Hawaii, and I hope he won't mind my quoting from the letter: "That week meant more to me than anything I have ever known. I am supposed to be a man, but every time I think of you I feel like crying. Silly, isn't it? But I love you and can't wait to see you again."

I got several hundred, sometimes thousands, of letters a week. None of them ever meant more to me. The reader will, I hope, excuse my sentimentality, but every time I think of Jim, I feel like crying too.

Not long after Jim returned to duty, another wonderful thing happened. This one brought the largest of my personal worries to an end. On June 1, 1966, I flew to Lansing, Kansas, and went out to the prison. The warden greeted me and then left me alone outside the locked gates.

When those locked gates next opened, Ezra Kingsley stepped through them. His scarred face scowling, he held out his hand to me.

And then he grinned, and he wasn't ugly at all any more.

Chapter 22

A sign along the road said I was leaving town, and as soon as I saw it I began to sweat, though it was certainly not hot. My hands were clammy, and from time to time I wiped them on my handkerchief.

The town we had left was San Francisco. The place we were going to was San Quentin. It's twenty miles from the city to the prison. San Quentin is on a peninsula and is mostly surrounded by water—which makes it hard for anyone who might somehow have made it over the wall to get much farther. The site was not picked by accident.

We covered those twenty miles all too fast for my taste. Within what seemed only minutes of leaving San Francisco, the car was nearing the massive edifice of steel and concrete surmounted by gun towers that is San Quentin. When we arrived, our escort turned to me and said "Come on." None of us was very conversational. One never is, on the way to a prison.

We walked up to the big locked gate—the same gate that closed on me a quarter of a century or so ago—and waited to be admitted. With my companion at my side, our escort behind us, I began to tremble and I tried to conceal my tension. I thought of turning back, but they were waiting for me in there.

And then I realized that what I felt was nothing compared to what Ezra, standing tense but composed at my right, must be going through. His twelve years straight time at Lansing were only days behind him, and the tight, sick sensation I get walking into a joint must be nothing compared to his feelings. Our escort was Warden Duffy, who was with us to address the new Seventh Step class at San Quentin. He discreetly looked away from us. He, too, understands.

A man who has once been a convict has his viewpoint twisted. Never again can such a man walk through a barred gate into a prison without painful recollections.

I glanced again at Ezra and his face was a rigid mask. And then the second of our Seven Steps flashed through my mind, and I wondered if, perhaps, he was thinking of it, too.

Realizing that there is a power from which we can gain strength, we have decided to use that power.

A guard appeared, and the gate swung open. I took a deep breath and stepped through it.

Printed in the USA
CPSIA information can be obtained
at www.ICGtesting.com
JSHW012021140824
68134JS00033B/2814

9 781722 501075

THE PATH
TO RICHES
IN THINK AND
GROW RICH